CANAL TOWN
YOUTH

SUNY series, Power, Social Identity, and Education
Lois Weis, editor

CANAL TOWN YOUTH

Community Organization and the Development of Adolescent Identity

JULIA HALL

State University
of New York
Press

Published by
State University of New York Press, Albany

Production by Susan Geraghty
Marketing by Fran Keneston

Printed in the United States of America

For information, address State University of New York Press,
90 State Street, Suite 700, Albany, NY 12207

Library of Congress Cataloging-in-Publication Data

Hall, Julia.
  Canal Town youth : community organization and the development of adolescent identity / Julia Hall.
     p. cm. — (SUNY series, power, social identity, and education)
  Includes bibliographical references and index.
  ISBN 0-7914-4813-4 (alk. paper) — ISBN 0-7914-4814-2 (pbk. : alk. paper)
     1. Socially handicapped teenagers—Education (Middle school)—Social aspects—United States—Case studies. 2. Middle school students—Social conditions—United States—Case studies. 3. Self in adolescence—United States—Case studies. 4. Gender identity—United States—Case studies. 5. Community education—United States—Case studies. I. Title. II. Series.

LC4069.3 .H37 2000
373.18—dc21

                                                          00-026527

10 9 8 7 6 5 4 3 2 1

This book is dedicated to my husband,
Robert Hall

CONTENTS

ACKNOWLEDGMENTS

Through the course of this project, there have been many people who helped me in immeasurable ways. Thank you Lois Weis for being a wonderful advisor and friend throughout graduate school. Susan Geraghty, thank you for being a patient and understanding editor. Angela Stevenson, Barbara Shircliffe, Amira Proweller, Illana Lane, Laura Meyers, Lynn Shaner, and Craig Centrie also deserve tremendous thanks for their warm friendship and intellectual guidance. The support of my siblings is always appreciated; thank you Elizabeth, Anne, and William Marusza, and Catherine Rakowski. A special thank you is extended to my nieces and nephews—Elizabeth, Peter, and Robert Rakowski, and Mary Marusza—for always making me laugh. I would like to acknowledge my late mother, Mary Marusza, who was not able to see this book in its completed form, yet her constant love and support is still with me and is one of the greatest gifts I have ever received. Thank you Robert Marusza, for being a terrific father, and for teaching me all about courage. Robert Hall, thank you, quite simply, for being my husband. Finally, thank you youth of Canal Town. I am humbled by your stories and inspired by your strength.

CHAPTER 1

Introduction

On the corner of a busy intersection in Canal Town stands the local community center.[1] A three-story brick building, the structure is architecturally unassuming, yet it stands out in the neighborhood in that the grounds are meticulously kept—bushes are trimmed, the small plot of grass is mowed, and the street gutters are not lined with trash. While half of the building functions as the community center, the other half is rented by a small meat-packing plant. Traffic hurdles by out front on busy Port Avenue—one of many commercial and commuter corridors that, along with the State Thruway, eventually connects the downtown area to a number of suburban western towns. Even though it is 2:45 P.M., and the K–8 bilingual school has just let out, the hurried drivers of the cars headed to suburban destinations after the workday do not stop to notice the stirrings of youth.

With its gutted warehouses, rusting grain elevators, and boarded-up homes and businesses, the neighborhood, which is fully economically dispossessed, represents a testament to urban blight and decay to many suburban dwellers. Today, the shattered glass, rusting metal, and rat-infested factories that litter the community are well explored by local youth, and are the sites of many accidents. Last summer, for example, a local boy drowned while diving off the top of an old grain elevator into the canal. Even though a postindustrial shadow hovers over this neighborhood, local poor white youth remain inured to the relationship between deteriorating conditions in their lives and the demise of industry.

At the juncture of ideology, structure, and culture, adolescent identity production involves a complex process whereby youth engage in the symbolic labor of constructing meaning through discursive social practices. Contextualized in a postindustrial economy, in this book, I explore the construction of gendered identities among a group of eighteen poor white middle school youth inside and across the K–8 bilingual school and the community center, both located in Canal Town. Here, I focus on the co-production of identities among these youth at the bilingual school, which serves students who are white, Puerto Rican, and, to a small extent, of African descent; and at the community center, which is largely patronized by poor Irish American neighborhood residents.

A definition of identity that underpins this investigation is the symbolic labor of constructing a sense of self inscribed with value through competing symbolic and material lived social practices. Such social practices are considered to be discursively produced in relation to the social structures that organize relations of power (Weedon, 1987; Wexler, 1988), with individuals as at least partial agents in the creation of their own forms of meaning (Carnoy, 1988). I understand identity, furthermore, as multiple and changing conceptions of self, whereby meaning is forged along points of individual and collective experience, social institutions, and economic structures which mediate the dialectical production of notions of race, ethnicity, class, and gender (Hicks, 1981; Crenshaw, 1989; McCarthy, 1990). I also rest my research upon the belief that institutionally inscribed relations of power are socially and historically constructed, and were created to benefit some over others (Ani, 1994). The construction of urban poor white adolescent identities in this analysis, therefore, will be emphasized as produced within history.

I demonstrate how urban *poor* white youth situated in a postindustrial economy and with historical connections to working class life negotiate identities within the spaces of their community. Up until now, this group has not been looked at in the literature. But as economic retrenchment becomes even more invasive in the lives of those urban residents who struggle to earn a living, more and more people are being forced into lives of poverty, or an "underclass" (Wilson, 1990). With the cutting of welfare, the nature of life in poor families is arguably beginning to change. In order to take part in the shaping of responsive public policy, it is crucial for educators to understand how poor youth from various cultural backgrounds make sense of their world. Although still socially and economically privileged by their whiteness, among former white workers, a family wage, for the most part, has disappeared, and the cushion of wealth that white laborers were often able to amass for their families across generations is beginning to deteriorate (Oliver & Shapiro, 1995). In this context, I document how poor white youth understand their economic dislocations. Middle school youth are at an ideal age for exploring these issues (Everhart, 1983; Finders, 1996). At a stage in life in which they are leaving childhood for their teenage years, many may be beginning to make decisions about what they want in the future.

This ethnography looks at the construction of adolescent identity as it is co-produced in *two* sites—the school and the community center. In this way, I explore a multidimensional sense of contradiction, struggle, and mediation in the formation of urban poor white adolescent identities. The importance of looking at multiple sites in the search for fuller understandings of adolescent meaning making is just starting to establish a presence in the literature (Heath & McLaughlin, 1983; McLaughlin, Irby, & Langman, 1994; Borman, 1998; Brown & Theobald, 1998; Muller & Frisco, 1998; Newman, 1998; Schneider & Stevenson, 1999). In addition to the school, by spending considerable time in the community center, I find it is a space the poor white youth designate as important, and which they setup as a place of safety and belonging in response to what they think to be trouble in school, at home, and on the streets. Through the collaborative and mobilization efforts of employees at the community center, networks are forged with a diverse group of external agencies, which ultimately works to sustain neighborhood goals. If the analysis was focused solely on the school, I would likely not have pickedup on this set of circumstances.

Existing investigations on the impact of formal and informal community-based agencies mostly evidence positive impact on school achievement and the production of adolescent identity (Heath & McLaughlin, 1983; McLaughlin, Irby, & Langman, 1994; Borman, 1998; Brown & Theobald, 1998; Muller & Frisco, 1998; Newman, 1998; Schneider & Stevenson, 1999). In the case of Canal Town, however, I argue that *negative* attitudes and behaviors are transmitted by the community center, which are then further elaborated on in the school. It seems the ideology of anger and blame embedded in the rhetoric of larger, national discourses, such as that of the New Right, is funneled into the community center, where it is somehow made understandable and meaningful to youth. In order to push these findings theoretically deeper, I think through the concept of "free space," as put forth by Evans and Boyte (1992). As will be investigated, the space of the community center diverges from that of Evans and Boyte as it is a space organized by adults for youth, and is a site in which the larger political project is the reification of whiteness. To this end, in this study of poor white adolescent identity formation, I both borrow and problematize the notion of "free space," and detail the inventive ways in which the white Canal Town youth are learning to produce the ideology of white supremacy inside this location.

REVIEW OF THE SOCIOLOGY
OF EDUCATION LITERATURE

In order to further understand how the intersectionality between the school and the community center in Canal Town may impact urban poor white adolescent identity formation, some sociology of education literature concerned with meaning-making processes among youth must be surveyed. This overview highlights the development of how identities are understood to be formed in schools in the sociology of education field. The review begins with a brief analysis of a structuralist framework, after which I explore how this led to the development of critical cultural theories of identity creation. The implications for critical cultural studies and the formation of gendered identities as culturally constructed in schools is then examined in order to set the backdrop for this book.

Social Reproduction Theory

In the main, conceptualized in the sociology of education literature in the United States in the early 1970s, is that student identities are linked to social and economic reproductive theory. Put forth in social and economic reproductive theory is the notion that schools reproduce social structures of inequality. Bowles and Gintis (1976) offer what some consider a seminal structuralist critique of the origins of disparity among social classes based on the organization of U.S. schools in a capitalist economy. In what they term the "theory of correspondence," Bowles and Gintis assert that schools function to reproduce class structures and the social relations of production based on the inequitable distribution of power in a capitalistic order.

Absent in reproductive studies is an exploration of the internal logic of school organization as it relates to concrete social interaction in the classroom. In the social reproduction literature, schools are not seen as cultural systems built upon a material and discursive field where institutional structures, symbolic systems, and actual social practices intersect in the complex construction of subjectivities (Roman, Christian-Smith, & Ellsworth, 1988). While Bowles and Gintis (1976) do not specifically focus on identity production in their work, in terms of their analysis, it follows that identities form in relation to school structures and largely reflect the hierarchical arrangement of class relations. The school, in the work of Bowles and Gintis, is simply an uncontested site for the reproduction of subjectivities.

Bowles and Gintis' (1976) reproductive theory casts identity formation in class-based terms that yield thin analyses of identity constitution devoid of dynamic historical social processes (McCarthy, 1988). With the focus on the structural imbalances that schools reproduce, structuralists such as Bowles and Gintis overlook potential modes of resistance that might emerge in response to structural inequality and the contradictions implicit in social relations in a capitalist society (Apple, 1982). This omission points to the fact that the construction of identities at the level of individual and collective social formation is disregarded entirely. In this early reproduction theory, structure instead of individual and collective agency programs identity. Not only do reproductive frameworks fail to provide a critique of social relations in the classroom as constitutive of identity production, the isolation of social class disregards the notion that race, ethnicity, class, and gender are interlocking systems inscribing forms of domination.

Critical Cultural Studies

Critical cultural theorists abdicate the notion that identities are fixed forms that are passively manufactured. By putting forth the notion of "culture," critical culturalists recognize semiautonomy in the construction of subjectivity and relations with others (Roman, Christian-Smith, & Ellsworth, 1988). These theorists view identities as formed in the fluid passageways between cultural texts, or symbolic meanings and lived social practices, and the social structures that buttress historically manufactured relations of domination and subordination (Omi & Winant, 1994). In the critical cultural model, race, ethnicity, class, and gender are concepts that are synthesized as texts, and resultantly, exist in material and symbolic form. As cultural texts, meanings, symbols, and ideologies are circumscribed and animated anew in everyday life (Smith, 1988). As constituted in historically rooted discursive and material social practices, in a critical cultural perspective, cultural systems are constructed intertextually through mutable struggles and contestations in the local site of everyday interaction (Roman, Christian-Smith, & Ellsworth, 1988).

Identity Construction:
Intersecting Race, Ethnicity, Class, and Gender

Unlike the earliest critical cultural ethnographies, which mostly did not consider the inner workings of school organization and the presentation of knowledge (Willis, 1977), today educational institutions are understood to provide significant sites for the production of youth cultural forms and identities (Weis, 1990). In order to understand some of the internal debates in the literature, Willis' work, which suggests schools promote both the reproduction and production of student subjectivities, is first explored. Later research in which class and gender are considered as the primary lens with which to view identity formation is then examined, followed by an overview of literature that views race as the focal point in the formation of student subjectivities.

Willis (1977) presents one of the earliest challenges to mechanistic reproduction theory. This study of how British male working class identity is, in part, formed in school, centers on white "lads" in the industrial English midlands. Willis' research evidences that schools are sites for both the reproduction and production of identities. Through discursive and material practices, Willis documents how the lads do not merely accept and internalize the messages in the school, but instead enact opposition to the symbolic and material forms of formal school culture. The lads' opposition to school culture includes rejecting mental labor, which they see as feminine, and the creation of a counterculture of resistance in school with roots in the shopfloor culture of their fathers and older brothers. Constantly trying to act adult, the lads form their identity around the male labor jobs they hope to hold in the future. By rejecting intellectual labor, the lads discount the possibilities of critical thinking as a tool for social transformation and subsequently reproduce themselves as a class. With few academic skills, the lads partially relegate themselves to the bottom because they close off access to higher paying and higher status jobs.

By showcasing the lads' culture of resistance, Willis (1977) reveals that schools are sites of contradiction and conflict in the formation of subjectivities. In hindsight, it can be argued that Willis' research does not magnify connections among school structures, knowledge and practices, and individual and collective modes of resistance. Although Willis uncovers how the lads create a sense of self in relation to white females and those from other cultural orientations, race, ethnicity, and gender are not seen as part of a holistic system in the construction of identity. White female and male and female identities from other cultural orientations in Willis' study, moreover, are positioned as dependent upon male subjectivity in white working class culture.

In the early 1980s, particularly socialist feminists began to seriously confront the suggestion in work such as Willis' (1977) that only white male cultures had a tradition of resistance (McRobbie, 1978; Valli, 1988). These socialist feminists place at the fore of their analysis the notion that class structures under capitalism and the organization of sex and gender relations are fused to a core mechanism of male domination and female subordination. Schools, however, are seen as sites for the potential reassemblage of gender and class relations. Critical ethnographic work on identity formation among white female adolescents indicates that young white women are, in some cases, at least partial agents in the construction of their own subjectivities. McRobbie's (1978) research on white working class female youth countercultures in the United Kingdom reveals that a group of girls who participate in a school-based youth club construct what seems to be an anti-school culture comprised of the adoption of material and symbolic forms of the culture of Western femininity. McRobbie's work indicates that these females do not simply allow their identities to be filled in with messages from the school and larger social structures. Instead, they actively reject formal school culture and preoccupy themselves with a cultural mode of opposition, with an emphasis on clothes, boys, and marriage.

Through this research, McRobbie (1978) finds that there are contradictions in the white working class girls' "production" of identity, as the formation of a culture of femininity is contingent upon the partial rejection of oppressive ideologies inscribed in white male privilege. In the end, McRobbie concludes that the emergence of reformulated gender and class identities among white working class young women do not, in their case, result in a redistribution of gender and class privilege. Even though these females respond to the material constraints that emerge from their class culture, similar to Willis' (1977) lads, they form an ethos that works to undergird the very structures of domination that have seemingly locked in their class and gender subordination.

The notion that schools are paradoxical locations for the construction of subjectivities is reflected in Valli's (1988) work on white working class female identity formation in a high school cooperative education program. Valli highlights the surfacing of identities surrounding notions of work and family in the context of participation in a clerical work curriculum. With the stated goal of the program being to put more women into stable, skilled jobs, Valli details how, in actuality, the enacted curriculum and teacher-student interaction seals in the subordinate working identities of white women. For these young females, school structures, knowledge, and practices work to dissuade them from academic subjects. In such a way, the students in Valli's study participate in the reproduction of gender roles by choosing a curriculum that diminishes the social and economic power of their labor identities in the private and public spheres of work.

In Weis' (1990) critical investigation of identity formation among white working class male and female "Freeway" high school juniors in a deindustrializing city, the impact of economic retrenchment on the meaning-making processes of teenagers is seriously considered. Weis finds the white working class Freeway males, in part, develop a sense of identity by directing anger toward others. As Weis explains, these young men are aware that the hard labor or "male" jobs which in the past defined for working class men a sense of their own masculinity no longer exist. When asked where they see themselves in the future, they place themselves in a domestic framework, where they retain a sense of manhood by emphasizing the male dominant structure of the larger culture. These males are angry at themselves for their devalued status, and, according to Weis, in talking about their futures, they displace their rage toward others—namely white females and males of African American descent. On the other hand, what is called a "moment of critique" surfaces in relation to how the Freeway females construct subjectivity. Not only do these white working class girls put an emphasis on further education, but most envision their futures in terms of jobs and careers, and therefore, do not seemingly form their identities around a domestic future. Weis reasons that at this point in time, paid work appears central in the construction of white working class female identities.

The construction of identities in schools around notions of race and ethnicity has received scarce treatment from educational researchers of the dominant Western culture (Willis, 1977; McRobbie, 1978; Valli, 1988; Weis, 1990). Both outside and inside university analyses are traditions of scholarship authored by those from culturally oppressed groups who have long pointed to race as historically shaped categories around which subjectivities are created to preserve power relations that benefit those of European ancestry over those from majority cultures (Woodson, 1933; Bryan, Dadzie, & Scafe, 1985; Ani, 1994). Bryan, Dadzie, and Scafe (1985) document the history of African Caribbean women living in the United Kingdom and their role as laborers, challengers, organizers, and preservers of culture. In examining the British education system, Bryan, Dadzie, and Scafe concur that while gender and class subordination limit females from reaching their personal and professional potentials, it is race that has the most significant influence on how identities are shaped—dictating which schools children can attend, the quality of their education, and their actual and internalized sense of placement within larger structures.

Bryan, Dadzie, and Scafe (1985) argue that children from culturally dominated groups are being systematically oppressed by the individual and institutionalized racism of British schools and teachers, and by the racist assumptions of a European-centered curriculum. In response, the authors describe how, in some cases, Saturday and other supplementary schools have been established for these children. These classes, taught by the mothers of African Caribbean children, center on teaching African Caribbean history and culture in addition to traditional British academic studies. These working class women, who often labor in service sector jobs to support their families, find time to organize and teach in order to invest their children with cultural pride, academic fluency, and the critical skills needed to confront and combat racism.

Other researchers document the fact that school structures are built upon the foundation of white privilege (Carrington, 1983; Polite, 1994). Carrington (1983), for instance, examines how West Indian boys and girls in a British high school are overwhelmingly "tracked" onto the athletic field, as compared to white youth, at the expense of academics. White teachers interviewed were of the opinion that sports was an appropriate forum for West Indian students, as they were thought to have superior physical skills and limited higher-ordered thinking capabilities. In this way, argues Carrington, the school is promoting the reproduction of West Indian youth into the lowest end of employment. Perhaps more important, the institution is also encouraging these children to internalize such stereotypes. In another example, Polite (1994) contends that African American male high school students view schooling in various ways, from accepting to highly critical. From "active conformists" to "overt resisters," Polite finds many youth in his study reproduce their social class status by discounting mental work in favor of peer culture. As these students narrate the belief that many of their teachers do not seem to care about their well-being, the school must be seen as promoting such outcomes.

Scholars of the dominant culture in U.S. academe are now beginning to examine "whiteness" in relation to identity formation processes (Frankenberg, 1993). In large measure, asserts Frankenberg, the voices of those from culturally oppressed groups have been diffused and marginalized through a "colonial discourse" that inscribes privilege by sustaining systematic domination of "others" in opposition to the Western white self. As being white is the condition of those who occupy the center, states Frankenberg, interrogating what that means necessitates that one dislodge what has historically been unmarked, precisely because of its centered location. As stated, ethnographic studies on the construction of white adolescent peer cultures along lines of class and gender have left relatively unexplored the constitutive dimension of race (Willis, 1977; McRobbie, 1978; Valli, 1988; Weis, 1990). While existing research focuses on white youth, the racial referent "white" is not decoded by those of the dominant culture for the very reason that it has been socially and historically centered and erased.

As seen in this review, studies of working class youth tend to dominate ethnographic analyses of identity formation (Willis, 1977; McRobbie, 1978; Carrington, 1983; Bryan, Dadzie, & Scafe, 1985; Valli, 1988; Weis, 1990; Polite, 1994). As the scholars of this research demonstrate, schooling does not do much to disrupt the reproduction of working class adolescent subjectivities. While Weis (1990) explores the effects of a deindustrializing economy on the lives of urban white working class high school students in the 1980s, it is important to call into question how such adolescents may be faring today. Although Fine and Weis (1998) analyze the construction of indentities among urban poor and working class adults from across racial and ethnic groups to see what their lives have been like since high school, the lives of poor urban *children* living in neighborhoods that have been *fully* economically dispossessed have not been considered. The only existing work which does focus on poor youth looks at rural culture (Borman, Mueninghoff, &

Piazza, 1988; DeYoung, 1995).[2] To fill this gap, here I explore how urban poor white middle school girls and boys construct identities in the spaces of a postindustrial urban community.

In this research, I understand social class as individual and collective relationships to the means of production (Sennett & Cobb, 1972; Halle, 1984). Based upon the words of the director of the community center and the principal of the school, and most important, the narrations of the youth themselves, I conclude that these are poor adolescents, who have historical connections to working class life, for instance, in terms of employment and education.[3] Throughout this analysis, the articulations and observations of these poor white youth are considered in the context of today's postindustrial economy.

By a postindustrial economy, I refer to the systematic disinvestment in the basic productive capacity of a nation, a trajectory acutely experienced in the United States during the 1970s and 1980s. During this time, the U.S. steel industry began a rapid decline, as did other areas of manufacturing and production, followed by the demise of businesses that were an outgrowth of larger industry. Bluestone and Harrison (1982) describe the process of deindustrialization as the diversion of financial resources, plants, and equipment from productive investment in basic national industries into speculation and shutdowns, lucrative global mergers and acquisitions, and foreign investment. Left in the shadow of global economic restructuring are derelict factories and displaced workers. It seems that overnight, the ability to make a decent living has closed shop and moved away. Canal Town is the oldest section of a city that fell victim to this shift toward an international market economy. By the latter half of the decade of the 1990s, urban communities such as Canal Town were populated with residents unable to find work (Perry, 1996). Likely enhanced by the costs of child care, transportation, and the lack of benefits outweighing the wages earned in service sector work, as described by the youth, most residents of Canal Town depend upon a variety of forms of public assistance, such as food stamps, Aid for Dependent Children (AFDC), and so forth.[4]

Scholars of recent literature in the sociology of education have left relatively unexplored the link between the school and other institutions. Those researchers who conducted earlier work in which they did consider other institutions, such as the family, focus on the lives of males from various cultural orientations, but do not directly look at how identities are being discursively constructed in multiple locations (Foote, 1943; Liebow, 1967; Thomas, 1967; Robins & Cohen, 1978; MacLeod, 1987; Walker, 1987). Today, many articulate that adolescents form identity in a variety of places, for instance, in school, at home, in places of worship, and with friends (McCarthy, 1990). As schools are just one site in the socialization of youth, when researchers focus only on that institution in considering the construction of identities, they lose sight of how other sources of socialization both encourage and contradict processes of meaning making. Lareau (1989) raises this point in a study of social class and parent involvement in schooling. Although not providing an analysis of identity formation, Lareau argues that parent impact on the lives of children is not relinquished as soon as youth step foot outside the front door.

By focusing on the production of urban poor white adolescent identities as constructed in school *and* other spaces which *they* designate as important, a deeper and more textured understanding of how youth make sense in their lives emerges. It is, perhaps, not surprising that the local community center is positioned by the white youth of Canal Town as a place of such importance. Today, with the convergence of the postindustrial economy; retreating public resources; and institutionalized racism, sexism, and homophobia, urban youth from various cultural orientations are seeking out in neighborhood organizations a sense of community not found on the streets and in schools (Heath & McLaughlin, 1983; McLaughlin, Irby, & Langman, 1994; Borman, 1998; Brown & Theobald, 1998; Mueller & Frisco, 1998; Newman, 1998; Schneider & Stevenson, 1999). Growing up in a city that has been ravaged economically, the white youth in Canal Town, for the most part, narrate lives plagued with poverty, violence, and, in their opinion, a school that does not seem to care. As the data reveal, these youth feel pushed out of their homes and the bilingual school, and they speak of the local community center as a "safe" and alternative location to those spaces in their lives which they do not find hospitable.

Current research on poor and working class urban populations reveals that adults are searching out "safe spaces" in the context of urban despair (Fine & Weis, 1998). Fine and Weis raise the question of the role of public space in the way poor and working class men and women strategize to shape their lives. The individuals in their study narrate home and public lives saturated with poverty, violence, and denigrating representations of race, ethnicity, class, gender, and sexuality. Even though their struggles are similar to those taken up by social activists in the 1960s and 1970s, the participants are detached from such movements, and in the case of the white informants, are highly critical. At the same time, those interviewed are also "homesteading," or seeking out material and spiritual places in their lives in which they can relieve themselves from daily duress. These places, argue Fine and Weis, although hidden from the intrusion of the larger public, are not simply geographical, but are sites in which social arrangements are politically challenged. The African American church, for example, is such a space in which individuals find communion and are producing counter-hegemonic representations of self in reinvisioning the future. Inside these places, explain Fine and Weis, people are collectively working to disengage from historically inscribed stereotypes, and are constructing new identities that both contest and confirm the structures which they inhabit.

While there is not much work specifically written on the use of public space in the construction of adolescent identities, similar to Fine and Weis (1998), as mentioned, I draw upon the notion of "free space" as forwarded by Evans and Boyte (1992). Evans and Boyte understand "free space" as the terrain between private lives and institutional structures, where citizens learn to critically assess their surroundings and work toward changing things for what they assume to be a common, democratic end. In these political settings, people learn organizational skills while forging a strong group identity among individuals with diverse perspectives, and where openness and debate prevail. In these spaces, connections, furthermore, are made to broader patterns of decision making, social life, and institutional practice. According to the authors, the meshing of local and larger patterns of society permits people to consciously construct goals for change.

However, as it relates to how the poor white Canal Town youth position and use the local community center, I both borrow and problematize the concept of "free space" (Evans & Boyte, 1992). While Evans and Boyte offer a model for collective action, they do not account for those sites which are seemingly "free," but which actually constitute spaces in which people from varying backgrounds work together toward shaping goals and identities they might *think* are democratic, but which are largely hegemonic and oppressive. Moreover, as Evans and Boyte do not consider spaces that are organized by adults for youth, their analysis remains limited for understanding how those who are older put together explanations of their social realities for themselves and their children. As the data in this research indicate, the Canal Town community center is arguably involved in a dialectical agenda focused on the elaboration and reification of whiteness and the denigration of "others." By looking at such sites, it can be seen how oppressive community ideology develops and is encouraged across generations. It also becomes clear that in arming children with particular critiques targeted at society, the poor white youth of Canal Town are being led to envision a sense of hope for the future in highly narrow and hegemonic ways.

As evidenced in this book, those interested in social transformation must think about life beyond the school in trying to understand how youth produce identities. By entering into the Canal Town community center—a space where poor individuals go to find a sense of relief and belonging—a wellspring of dreams percolate into action. Through the conscious efforts of white adults, it can be seen that in this space, children are learning to rely upon both their own resources and those of others from varying agencies and institutions in order to strengthen a racist agenda. In this way, the community center can be viewed as a literal white "construction site," where the scaffolding that supports and sustains white supremacist ideology is both produced and encouraged within children, within the neighborhood, across communities, and across generations.

By looking at the history of Canal Town, it becomes clear that white racism toward those from culturally oppressed groups has existed even in times of relative prosperity. Today, however, with few connections left to the Civil Rights movement and the retreat of labor unions—and aided by contemporary conservative rhetoric—inside the community center, the poor white youth of Canal Town are learning to galvanize resources in order to assert a sense of white supremacy. Although these actions are likely in response to their presently impoverished lives, the elaboration of racism is not a product of a restructuring economy, but has much deeper historical beginnings (Ani, 1994). Certainly not all white working class and poor youth and adults display racist and sexist attitudes and behaviors. Research demonstrates how white working class youth, for example, are found to be "bordercrossers," pro-Chicanos, and "wanabees" (Foley, 1990; Peshkin, 1991; Seeley Bordon, 1998). The residents of Canal Town, however, are from a certain segment of the white poor and working class. Their processes of meaning making are a function of a very particular social and economic history.

CANAL TOWN

In order to gain a sense of the complex nature of the process of identity formation among the poor white youth in this book, it is critical to examine the historical development of the formerly white working class community of Canal Town. The construction of identities among Canal Town residents parallels, and is deeply entrenched in, the economic and demographic history of the area. The history of Canal Town has much to say about the current economic, political, and social life of the neighborhood, and in particular, the solidarity of the community.[5] Although hostility toward the Anglo American industrial elite remains present in this Irish American community, such anger will be seen to be deflected onto those from culturally oppressed groups during the formation of an Irish working class identity.

Stories of the Irish people in this part of the city are legacies that have been passed down from one generation to the next. Older residents of Canal Town continue to contend that the Irish workers were responsible for the single biggest event that drove the economy of the area for years—digging the last stop on the Midwestern Canal. Irish American families in Canal Town arguably remain the custodians of history in that part of the city. This is perhaps why the district is still, despite changing demographics, so caught up in the Irish experience. In this historical look at the Irish presence in Canal Town, I rely upon secondary histories, primary documents, and the words and recollections of three former residents of the area—Dusty, Patrick, and Carolyn. Of these informants, Dusty and Carolyn are over the age of 85, are of Irish descent, and were interviewed individually in their homes. According to these longtime residents, the Irish people never really asked for much in terms of compensation or recognition of their efforts, yet time and again have been exploited and used. As Carolyn exclaims, "Growing up in Canal Town, you heard a lot of stories about like, 'Oh, we built this place; we opened-up _____ [the city], and now look at what we get.'" By exploring aspects of this history it can perhaps be seen how and why the Irish in this community, and in the city at large, remain such a tight-knit group.

During the construction of the canal across the state, which began in 1815, Irish immigrants found themselves in Canal Town, as it was the last stop on the project.[6] With the completion of the canal in 1827, many Irish workers and their families settled in Canal Town, establishing what came to be known by the Anglo-elite as the first ethnic neighborhood in the city. While Anglo Protestant merchants and traders directed the city's economic and political life, the Irish remained a ready source of inexpensive labor (Hill, 1908; Wittke, 1939, 1956). A few incoming Germans worked in surrounding industry, but eventually moved out of the densely Irish and Roman Catholic Canal Town, and opened up shops of their own. During this time, most Irish laborers worked in jobs that were associated with the loading and unloading of lake and canal boats, such as longshoremanship.[7] While the men worked hard and were poorly paid, the women took care of children and often did piecework out of their homes (Hubbell, 1896; Hill, 1923; Walter, 1958).

With the opening of the canal, a small influx of Italian, Polish, and more German and Irish immigrants began to come through Canal Town to buy provisions before heading out West. In many cases, after arriving with all their worldly possessions, it was allegedly commonplace for whole families to be robbed, and subsequently, be forced to stay.[8] Members of these groups eventually found work in taverns, hotels, and other industry that revolved around canal trade and transport. There was also a transient population coming through Canal Town, which included merchant seamen, tradespeople, and sales representatives (Maynard, 1908; Houghton, 1927; Schneider, 1938; Ellis, 1956). Up until 1845, Canal Town was bordered on the south by the Creek Reservation. During that year, white developers forced the Mohawk off the reservation and cleared the land for expansion. Some of the Mohawk went south to the Chicago Reservation, while others, who had been forced to convert to Christianity, according to historians, came to live on the outskirts of Canal Town (Hotchkin, 1848; Ketchum, 1865; Donohue, 1895; Devoy, 1896; Pedersen, 1956).

For at least the first thirty-five years after the Windsor Land Company took the land from indigenous peoples and opened it up for European settlement, about 90 percent of its citizens were of Anglo origin, while the remaining 10 percent were Irish and German. The Anglo "settlers" mainly took up residency in what was thought of as the city center. By 1850, 30 percent of the city's population were Roman Catholic Irish, and 30 percent were of Protestant German descent. The Germans were better educated and skilled than the existing Irish, Polish, and Italian immigrants who followed, and largely fared better economically and socially (Ellison, 1880; Wittke, 1939; Walter, 1958). Due to the high concentration of crime in Canal Town, and the economic expansion of the city, German, Italian, and Polish immigrants did not settle there. Italian Americans typically moved to the west of the canal, while Polish and German Americans moved south. The more prosperous members of the Irish community moved north, although they remained adjacent to Canal Town, where there was plentiful work (Johnson, 1879; Maynard, 1908; Houghton, 1927; Schneider, 1938; Ellis, 1956).

During the mid-1800s, a small group of people of African descent migrated to the city from Canada or the northeast, and settled on the south side of town, where they were surrounded by German residents. Men of African descent held general labor and skilled positions, but because their wages were considerably lower than those of whites, African women commonly took on jobs as domestics in the homes of the Anglo and rising German business class. Although, for a while, this metropolis was a center for some abolitionist and Free Soil political activity,[9] it was, like most cities in the United States, a place of intense racism directed toward those who were African.[10] While many whites appeared appalled at slavery, some workers' hostility toward the institution was driven by fear of having to compete with slave labor. Arguably, those of the business class also did not want to live among people of African descent.[11] Due to historically structured racism, Africans on the south side of town lived an increasingly segregated life (Hosmer, 1880; Poole, 1905; Severance, 1909).[12]

About a decade after the opening of the canal, Canal Town emerged as the economic hub of the western end of the state, and had a tough reputation to match. Historical documents describe Canal Town as a bustling post, crowded with sail and steam vessels, clusters of wooden houses, and brick and stone warehouses and stores. These texts, however, also refer to Canal Town as a "true frontier," where "boisterous" boatmen and seamen drank and brawled and where "women of the streets" pursued a lucrative trade (Police Annuals, 1838; Charity Organization, 1839; Symons & Quintus, 1902). Patrick captures that same type of atmosphere while describing an experience he had working for a butcher when he was 10 years old:

> I used to go in and clean the coolers out . . . scrape the butcher block, clean knives and saws and all that to make a few bucks. . . . This one guy used to come in the store every now and again and he looked ancient. He had to be in his 90s if he was a day, and he looked awful. I mean, he had pieces of his ear missing. I remember being terrified of him . . . he had the nastiest disposition. The guy used to walk down the street and dogs would bark. He used to come in the store, and I remember Jake [the butcher] would give him a sandwich, something to drink, a cup of coffee, and they would sit and chat. I remember asking Jake, "Who was this guy, and why is he so scary looking?" Jake explained that he was one of the "bottle gang" members, the last of the bottle gangs. . . . He [Jake] was telling me that back in the early to mid-nineteenth century, the canal district was still pretty wild. They used to have these bottle gangs that roamed around there and they would do anything for money in order to buy booze. Anything, including murder or to rob people for money, and there were a number of these gangs which used to roam around the canal district knocking people off. . . . In some taverns there was a trapdoor in the floor, where you could dispose of a body and it would go out into the canal, never to be seen again.

Patrick, Dusty, and Carolyn all recount similar stories about the existence of trapdoors during this time. As others document, in the 1830s, Canal Town housed saloons, dance halls, and establishments of "ill-fame" too numerous to count. Local accounts also report that some saloon keepers would drug patrons' drinks, rob them of their valuables, and dump them down a trapdoor into the canal (Poole, 1905; Schneider, 1938; Brown & Watson, 1981). City documents seemingly corroborate these accounts, as the police reported that they would regularly find bodies floating in the murky water (Police Annuals, 1838). While growing up, the Canal Town elders say they remember countless stories about how merchant seamen would pass through, and "grab somebody, and then steal and maybe murder them, and then be gone to Detroit the next day." It is worth noting that the contemporary violence and crime white Canal Town residents solely associate with African Americans and Puerto Ricans has such long-standing roots in their own community and is a boastful part of their collective memory.

According to city records, Irish and African workers clashed daily on the docks of Canal Town (Police Annuals, 1837, 1840, 1843). Playing on white people's historically inscribed sense of racism, capital continuously used Black labor to break strikes, with the likely intent of keeping a class consciousness from forming (Roediger, 1994). By the mid-1850s, "race riots" between Irish and African laborers had become reportedly "commonplace," and the business class attributed such action to the "aggressive" nature of both groups (Century Club, 1854, 1856; Charity Organization, 1855).

With the advent of the Civil War, a federal draft was imposed on the city in the summer of 1862. In order to fill the quota of soldiers needed from the city as mandated by the federal government, and, in order to avoid being drafted, the political and economic leaders of the city organized a monetary reward reportedly to bribe the poor to volunteer. While this enticement did not ultimately prevent a draft, it did enable most of the business and elite class and their families to escape the call to arms. During the summer of 1863, according to police reports, nearly one hundred Irish Canal Town laborers went on strike in protest against meager wages and enlisting buyouts. When their employers responded by hiring Black workers as strikebreakers, violence ensued (Police Annuals, 1863). Despite the rhetoric of the day that the Civil War was being fought over the issue of slavery, the Irish workers and others were reportedly angered that they were expected to give up their lives "to free" the very people who were breaking their strikes. In this way, although Irish laborers were angry at the Anglo American elite for exploiting their labor, many Irish people also displaced considerable rage on people with virtually no social or political power, positioning Africans as the ones who were also responsible for the white workers' oppression. The protest among the Irish workers on the docks is documented in public records to have suddenly turned into a mob march from Canal Town to the small African American neighborhood on the south side. During this summer afternoon, Irish marchers threatened many lives and killed one Black man (Police Annuals, 1862, 1863, 1864; Wittke, 1939, 1956).

The anger during the Civil War that emerged among the city's immigrant communities perhaps led to feelings of nationalism, particularly among the Irish community in Canal Town, where the Fenian Movement took strong hold. The primary objective of Fenianism was to capture Canada and hold it hostage until England surrendered Ireland. Developed as an idea in famine-stricken Ireland in the 1840s, it grew among the Irish immigrants inside the industrial urban centers of the United States, where many felt they were laboring hard to line the pockets of transplanted wealthy British. Many Irish people in Canal Town, and in other cities in the north, were incensed that the British had manipulated the potato famine of the 1840s as a method of starving the Irish in order to take over the land. The Canal Town Irish residents, historians speculate, projected their anger for the British on the Protestant elite of the city, whom they thought were also exploiting the Irish people for profit here in the New World (Police Annuals, 1862, 1863; Wittke, 1939, 1956).

At the end of the Civil War, according to Shamus O'Leary, an Irish worker and aspiring journalist, Canal Town residents felt that one result—the legal emancipation of Africans—would ensure a steady stream of cheap labor with whom they could not compete (1870). For the surviving thousands of Irish soldiers who were released from duty after the war with no compensation, the Fenian Movement was, perhaps, appealing. Due to the location of Canal Town and the strength of the local Fenian Brotherhood, the city was chosen as the national point of departure for the capture of Canada. With a date planned for invasion, thousands of Fenians from across the midwest came to the city and were put up in homes, taverns, and boarding houses throughout Canal Town and other northern sections of the city. Rumor had it that the Irish were stockpiling weapons. On the morning of June 2, 1866, over one thousand Fenian soldiers crossed the Falls River in boats, disembarking on the shores of Canada (Police Annuals, 1865, 1866). But because of their lack of provisions and their inability to travel any other way except by foot, the Fenians quickly announced defeat and went home. In the years to follow, Fenianism lost much of its fervor. Patrick and Dusty, however, tell me that there is still a strong anti-British sentiment in the neighborhood, and that in their lifetimes, they have heard of many benefits for the Irish Republican Army in Canal Town.

During this time, the city continued to expand, thriving on the merchant trade and grain industry—all made possible by the Midwestern Canal. Already a leading lake and canal port, the area soon became a center for the new rail transportation. Grain that was shipped to other areas in the midwest through the canal and the Great Lakes was stored in the massive Anglo- and German-owned grain elevators that lined the banks of Canal Town. After it was scooped into railroad cars by mostly Irish labor, it was then transported to points west and east via rail (Dart,

1879; Closson, 1894). The 1850s and 1860s were characterized by the extension of lines westward, which were rapidly expanded during the Civil War due to the necessary transport of goods. During this time, the population exploded with new members of current ethnic groups, and others—including Eastern European Jews, Ukrainians, and Canadians.[13] Growing numbers of people of African descent also began to arrive from the South during Reconstruction. These individuals also settled on the south side of town (Johnson, 1879; Maynard, 1908; Houghton, 1927; Schneider, 1938; Ellis, 1956).

The stage was set for the city's future position as a commercial world center for the manufacture and transport of steel (Common Council, 1895, 1897). Due to its status as a major port, the area emerged as a natural terminus for rail lines, connecting it with large steel markets out west and in Canada. By the end of the European 1914–18 War, the city had the reputation as an industrial giant, a global center for the production and movement of steel, railroad cars, automobiles, engines, and airplanes. For many decades, this industrialization created a climate in which great numbers of white unskilled male workers could bring home a comfortable family wage. With two steel plants in the vicinity of Canal Town, hundreds of small, bustling businesses continued to spring up.

Unrealized at the time, it was during the 1920s that the global trends that have come to signify the current economic crisis in this city first became apparent (Perry, 1995). While area politicians and leaders spoke proudly about an industrial stronghold, the commercial status of the city was beginning to tarnish, and in just a few decades, it would fade beyond recognition. During the Depression, many locally owned manufacturers went out of business. Although the European 1945–49 War brought industrial prosperity, in reality, it did not last. The opening up of the Madison Riverway in 1959, a direct water route between the Great Lakes and the Atlantic Ocean, quickly washed over the once thriving commercial economy of the city. With the disappearance of commerce, the city turned to its sole hope—steel. With the rest of the industrial world in Europe severely damaged by the war, cities in the United States, like this one, were able, for a time, to dominate global markets. By the end of the 1960s, however, Japan and Germany rebuilt, and with more advanced processes of steel manufacturing, rivaled industrial centers in the United States. Automation, consolidation, and the constant search for cheaper labor markets led corporate heads to shut down industries in the north. By the close of the 1970s, U.S. industries were on the demise, and cities such as the one in which Canal Town is located, followed this trend (Bluestone & Harrison, 1982; Perry, 1995).

Industrial deterioration and a growing African American and Puerto

Rican presence in the city affected the white populations of Canal Town and the surrounding urban environs. During the 1950s and 1960s, largely due to racial fear and the start of deindustrial decay, urban white residents sold or rented their homes and moved out to the suburbs—west and north of the city—at alarming rates. This flight began a trend in which remaining city residents overwhelmingly consisted of poorer and older individuals of European descent, and thousands of those of African descent on the south side. Incoming Puerto Ricans mainly settled on the east side of town (Brown & Watson, 1981; Perry, 1996). Structural racism continued to restrict these groups from the social and economic life of the city.

Changes were also taking place directly in Canal Town. The Pepper Projects, a low-income housing development that was soon populated with mostly African American residents, was contracted by the city to be built on the southwestern edge of this district. Due to the rise in violent crime and gang activity on the east side and the appeal of affordable housing in Canal Town, a steady stream of Puerto Ricans also began to move into Canal Town. The residents at the time, who were still largely Irish, contend Patrick, Dusty, and Carolyn, were angered by this intrusion into their community, prompting those with more resources to flee north of the city or the suburbs. Those who remained clung onto the last vestiges of industry, for example, explains Partick, working a few months in a carburetor factory until it closed, then moving on to an envelope company until the workers were laid off, and so forth. Today, Dusty says, most are not able to find any employment at all.

Although the Irish residents in Canal Town have historically been oppressed by capital, they have also been privileged by their whiteness. Unlike those from culturally oppressed groups, white Canal Town residents and those of the dominant culture elsewhere have historically been able to accumulate financial resources and build it into their families across generations. Of the former residents who were interviewed, Dusty and Carolyn are home owners. Privileged by race in terms of the ability to amass wealth, most of these citizens were able to inherit or buy property, pay it off, and pass it down to their children. Race privilege, as it relates to income, access to loans, better jobs, and so forth, has traditionally combined with the inheritance of transgenerational resources to secure the maintenance of a particular way of life (Oliver & Shapiro, 1995). Due to structural barriers, those of African and Puerto Rican descent, who are newcomers to Canal Town, have historically been denied access to financial resources, and the ability to accumulate and spread wealth across generations. One outcome is the seeming absence of a safety net to catch members of these groups when things get tough.

The oldest residents of Canal Town, who remember a time when things were different, count their losses in stories that revolve not so much around the loss of industry, but around being slighted by "City Hall," in that they think local officials are causing them to lose control of their community. Instead of blaming the capital elite for their economic dislocations, these residents direct anger toward low-level government officials whom they believe are allowing historically available "others" to step in and "take over." Dusty and Carolyn are angry about the demise of neighborhood institutions that have been built by generations of Irish people. As explained by these informants, places such as the school, church, and local taverns, and the sense of well-being inscribed within, have historically helped hardworking local families get through the day. In some cases, in the view of these residents, local government does not see whites as having much value, and therefore, such institutions are allowed to fall by the wayside.

Over twenty years ago, the K–8 bilingual institution in Canal Town used to be a neighborhood school. According to the Canal Town elderly interviewed, back when it served only local youth, to no avail, area residents had long asked City Hall to make improvements. Today, Carolyn is of the opinion that you have to be Puerto Rican in order to get the government to pay attention. Back in 1958, Carolyn remembers that community parents petitioned City Hall to improve the school's physical structure and safety measures. In the late 1960s, Carolyn relays that a student was using a grinding wheel in shop class when it exploded, killing the child. She remembers that residents of Canal Town had the attitude of "Look, what does it take to get attention to our school? We're lacking basic safety equipment and one of our kids just got killed, and nothing happened." They put a little money in the school, continues Carolyn, but nothing really happened until it was changed over to a bilingual institution. Carolyn recalls that people in the neighborhood were wondering, "Do we have to bring people from outside the neighborhood in order to get attention to our issues? Aren't we legitimate enough on our own?" Not only were Canal Town residents not consulted in making the decision to transform the school, says Carolyn, but existing teachers were reassigned, and Spanish-speaking teachers, administrators, and students from other communities were brought into the building. Thus, as Carolyn sees it, in one stroke, the institution's historical part of the Irish experience in the neighborhood was severed.

The Roman Catholic Church, as well, is no longer considered by Patrick, Carolyn, or Dusty to be a socially organizing force in Canal Town, largely due to religious leaders "brought in from the outside" who "have no vision for the old community." Dusty remembers how while he was growing up, the priest from the local Irish church used to walk through Canal Town, blessing houses, visiting the sick, and stopping by the taverns every Friday night for "a couple of beers, just to see what was going on in the neighborhood." Although it is an Irish church, built by Irish labor, Patrick criticizes the succession of priests during the past few decades for not living in Canal Town and for trying to attract wealthier parishioners from the larger city. As Patrick describes these changes, he views the current priest as handling matters in ways that are anathema to the people:

> So the priest's bringing in people from outside the area, and a lot of them have big cars, Mercurys and Cadillacs, and they were parking their cars in the church parking lot. A couple of them had been vandalized. So what does the priest do as a solution to that? He puts up these big fences, like 8-foot-high fences with barbed wire on the top, all around the church. People [white Canal Town residents] were going, "Oh my God, what an insult. How dare you do this; who do you think you are?"

Patrick, Dusty, and Carolyn all think back to a time when the church was open to the people and integrated with the community. These individuals have a strong sense of what the parish has meant historically to Canal Town, for instance, Dusty says, "it was always us, the poor, Catholic, Irish who were looked down upon by the Protestants in the rest of _____ [the city]. But we [Canal Town Irish] had our church. It was in our prayers, in the basement of that church, and the taverns, where we met and developed a tough fighting attitude. That's what kept us alive." Carolyn explains that priests are transients, they come and go, "but the church, to us [Canal Town people], we literally built that parish . . . the church belongs to us. How dare anyone put up barbed wire around the church."

Taverns, which represent a Canal Town institution that has also crumbled, apparently were much more than places to drink. As Patrick reminisces, it was common for these establishments to hold raffles to raise money for residents, for example, who was sick or down on their luck. At one time, maintains Patrick, "there was a tavern on every corner, and one in the middle of the block." According to the narrations of older residents, every tavern would be packed on Friday night for a fish fry, where entire families would go to be entertained by an upright piano. As Patrick describes, for a long time, the lunch trade did a fairly good business:

> Everybody worked for either _____ or _____ [steel plants], to the point where you had taverns that people would go to because they all worked the late shift at Gate 5. So they would all get together at one

time and one place . . . groups would form around work schedules. . . . In fact, you had taverns that would open up, and back when I was a kid I would wonder how they could be up all night. I remember walking to school in the morning and these guys would be getting out of 3rd shift at the steel plants, and they would be coming home all filthy, grungy, and they would go hit the tavern, at like, 7:30 in the morning, and they would be drinking beer and eating roast beef sandwiches.

Patrick describes that when he was in seventh grade, he used to make a fair amount of money in the taverns by drawing portraits, choosing this vocation because there was an oversaturation of young boys in the shoe-shine trade. He maintains he used to make his rounds from one tavern to the next in the course of a weekend night, until his last stop, where the cook always gave him a leftover fish fry and birch beer. When Patrick was older, he explains, he worked in the steel plants and became a part of that lunch and weekend crowd, as he remembers: "I used to sit in a tavern on Friday nights watching the street lights shining in the window and watching the trickles of the metal dust falling through the light and in the falling snow, and thinking how nice it looked . . . how pretty it was with all these sparkles." Today, there are only a handful of bars left in the area. Carolyn and Dusty report, however, that they are not places for families, pianos, and fish fries, but are host to heavy drug trafficking and alcohol abuse, most of which is "brought in by minorities."

In the early 1950s, City Hall and the State negotiated to build the State Thruway connecting suburban towns from the north and west of the city with downtown. The thruway was constructed to run between the eastern edge of Canal Town on one side, and downtown and the west side on the other. Again, Dusty states, not one Canal Town resident was consulted. This act, assert all of the interviewed residents, effectively cut Canal Town off from downtown. With the glory days of the Midwestern Canal long gone, downtown had become the economic lifeblood of Canal Town. As Dusty bitterly recounts, "Here you had communities of people who had been there for generations, working their tails off for the city, establishing their families, building social institutions in the area, and then they got rewarded by being selectively cut off from the rest of the city. If we were minorities instead of white, we'd get a lot better treatment." Being physically isolated from the city center for a few decades, there is a sense among Canal Town residents that they are forgotten by those whom they believe have the power to make improvements in their lives. In fact, says Patrick, if you talk to people in the city today, many do not even know where Canal Town is located.

These Canal Town residents articulate a sense of abandonment by the city. To them, it seems that everyone has developed a case of historical amnesia when it comes to remembering those who labored to open up the city to the world. Instead of blaming the capital elite for selling them out, Dusty and Carolyn continue to blame relatively low-level government officials, clergy, and "minorities." Even though those at City Hall likely do shape policy, the nature of such policy is controlled by a more powerful business elite that directs markets and the economy. It may be that a working class consciousness had been eroded to such an extent, that Dusty and Carolyn no longer think to "look up" in searching for someone to blame. Dusty reiterates this thinking when he reasons that the only people who appear to benefit from City Hall are those of African descent who live in the Pepper Projects, because "at least the projects got worked on. They did some rehabilitation work and it looks a lot better now, but it sure makes you wonder, do you have to be a minority to get assistance?" These anti-government sentiments and racial "othering" seemingly contribute to the maintenance of Irish conviviality, as does the actual isolation of the community.

Today, Canal Town is physically sectioned off from the rest of the city by derelict warehouses to the north, the State Thruway to the west, the Pepper Projects and overgrown railroad tracks to the south, and old grain elevators and the lake to the east. The total number of residents has dwindled, and the streets of Canal Town are characterized by boarded-up homes and "for rent" signs. Because of the heavy reliance on public assistance in the area, many of these white residents are losing their homes, some of which have been in their families for generations (Grant Agency Demographics, 1996). However, because there are, to some extent, cushions of accumulated resources still in place among the old Irish American families in Canal Town, if someone is evicted, they are less likely, for example, than someone of African descent, to end up on the street. Oftentimes there may be an older relative who can dip into a pension to make a loan, or who can take them in.

In this exploration of the history of Canal Town, I demonstrate how white racism toward those of African and Puerto Rican descent has always existed, even when there was work available in the community. As the elder white Canal Town residents complain today about violence and crime they believe to be brought into the neighborhood by those from culturally oppressed groups, they also, ironically, boast about the legacies of murder and gang violence which they narrate as a part of their own past. As the poor, but formerly working class white residents of Canal Town evidence that such displacements and white supremacist attitudes are part of their collective memories, they draw upon a sense of racism that is embedded much farther back in the bedrock of history (Ani, 1994).

I now turn to a chapter outline of this ethnographic investigation. In Chapter 2, I lay out the methodology used in this research, and provide background information on participants. By listening to the words of the poor white Canal Town youth, it is discerned they are presently poor but have historical connections to working class life. In Chapter 3, I detail the narrations and elaborations of the poor white Canal Town girls as they struggle to make sense of their lives at home, on the streets, at school, and at the Center. In Chapter 4, I chronicle how the poor white Canal Town boys articulate and animate notions of identity in these same locations. Through the narrations and actions of sixth, seventh, and eighth grade teachers, in Chapter 5, I examine how the bilingual middle school both promotes and contradicts the tendencies emerging within the identities of white Canal Town youth. In Chapter 6, I explore how the white youth set up the community center as an alternative space to home, the streets, and school. I also consider how poor white youth are encouraged by adults to use that space to collectively produce and elaborate upon whiteness. Summarizing these findings, in Chapter 7, I comment on the importance of continuing to understand such spaces.

CHAPTER 2

Entering the World of Canal Town

While the poor white youth of Canal Town tell the story of their lives, it is ultimately my hand that shapes them into this finished piece. As an ethnographer, I am aware of the influences of my own subjectivity in selecting research topics, designing projects, and collecting and analyzing data. Some argue that researchers bring two selves into any site: the human self, which reflects the way experiences are mediated; and the researcher self, which is constructed to fit the specific investigative situation. In qualitative analysis, the human self, which includes multiple and changing dispositions, is ever-present (Peshkin, 1986). Throughout this project I reflect upon my influence on the relationship between researcher and informants. Also considered is my authoritative position as a researcher and the placement of my own voice in the analysis (Ladson-Billings, 1994).

There are concerns specific to working in dispossessed communities which researchers have an obligation to consider. Bourgois (1995) reminds that any researcher who probes the lives of those who are socially marginalized confronts serious problems with respect to representation, particularly in relation to stereotypes of poverty and race. By looking into the lives of urban poor white middle school youth, I mainly confront dilemmas of representation in respect to poverty. Although concerned about the risks to those studied that are involved in the revealing of narrative, Bourgois states that editing the horrors which exist in impoverished urban neighborhoods would work to soften the social misery, and thus, link the researcher to the forces of oppression.

In the community in which I conducted this research, I saw most fathers were absent, while mothers, many of whom were intravenous drug users, could easily be criticized for exposing their children to narcotics, abuse, and child neglect. I often observed and heard white local politicians and social service workers who, upon visiting the Canal Town community center, would scan the neighborhood with shock and dismay, and denounce area parents for having large families, collecting welfare, and spending their checks on drugs while their children remain malnourished, dirty, and poorly dressed. Some of this shock and anger, it can be argued, may come from the fact that it is widely believed among the dominant culture that these problems only exist in African American communities. Nevertheless, I am aware the data in this ethnography might be misconstrued as an exposé about the problems with the welfare system and those who abuse it. In no way do I intend to imply this, or more seriously, that those who are poor are not good parents. Rather, for enough people to be incited toward social justice, I believe the minutia of daily life in communities such as Canal Town must be chronicled in raw detail.

Many ethnographers become intimately involved with the the people they study—and I am no different. The role of the researcher is emotionally difficult. It was often the case that in one moment I would pain for the poor white youth when I heard stories of abuse, only in the next, to be repulsed as they revealed a virulent sense of racism. While I do not hide my anger toward the violence which saturates these poverty-stricken young lives, nor toward their racism, I endeavor to create an historical, critical understanding of life in this traditionally white working class neighborhood. I consider how events and actions are dialectically produced between structures and people, in a particular moment in social and economic history. In this way, I attempt to demonstrate how adolescents are partial agents in the production of their own culture. Although my life has been quite different from that of the white youth of Canal Town, research in this community is important to me for both personal and political reasons.

I grew up in a northeastern city that was also seriously suffering the affects of the shift to a postindustrial economy. As the economic life of my hometown was also largely based upon the production and transport of steel, today former workers are facing lives of poverty. Due to historically based racism inscribed in institutions and the discourse of "lost entitlement" narrated among many white citizens, the city in which I was born is also highly segregated. While on break from graduate studies in the Sociology of Education, I was visiting a friend in another city for the summer when I took a job as a literacy instructor as part of a government sponsored program. I chose to do this because while studying theoretical issues in education at a large research university, I found I had little contact with youth. I worked as a tutor in community centers across the city when I first entered the world of Canal Town. The segregated nature of this northern city seemed familiar. During the following summer I also participated in the program, and was placed exclusively at the Canal Town center.

It was at the intersection of biography and exposure to theory that I began to develop a large-scale project in which I was to examine how urban poor white girls and boys construct gendered identities in a formerly white working class community. As a researcher and writer my vantage point is neither objective nor disinterested. I was well known in the community center before I began to think of it as a place to conduct a study. I had come to know the youth and their families fairly well. A part of me would like to think it was due to this familiarity that the youth and staff members openly shared with me, during formal interviews, the pain, happiness, frustration, and anger in their lives. In "truth," however, I am a middle-class university-educated female in my mid-20s who is simply a *visitor* in Canal Town. Due to social class and university connections, my presence in this neighborhood and my relations with people were based on an inequitable distribution of power. How this affects the interview and observational data and the entire construction of the project is unmeasurable, but likely profound.

Despite this dilemma, I feel that what the Canal Town residents say is important. By paying close attention to socially and historically encoded ways in which gender categories are formed and sustained today in a white community center and a K–8 bilingual school, both located in the same neighborhood, through the words and actions of participants, I hope to advance a deeper understanding of how urban poor white youth are making meaning in their lives in the context of a restructuring economy. Such knowledge, perhaps, is the first step toward dismantling a white supremacist system. I cannot, however, forget my powerful role in shaping data.

THE POLITICS OF ACCESS

Access is a social process that demands continous negotiation and renegotiation between researcher and field members throughout the duration of a study (Burgess, 1991). Part of the politics of ethnographic research, access is regulated throughout the data collection process as relationships change and develop on different levels across time. My access to the Canal Town Community Center as a research location was slightly unusual. Unlike some researchers, I did not formulate an investigation and then look for a corresponding site (Proweller, 1995; Meyers, 1996). Instead, the development of my question grew out of my experiences as a tutor at the community center in Canal Town. While helping youth with their schoolwork, I also got to know them on a personal level. I additionally began to notice some patterns of activity emerge.

What initially struck me about the Center[1] was that it was located in a multiethnic neighborhood, yet, in all but a few exceptions, I only saw white and a few Puerto Rican girls attend. Another interesting aspect was that every day, in small groups, those same local children—

from kindergarten through eighth grade—would walk directly to the Center after school and stay until quite late at night, often walking home alone in the dark. I observed that none of these children were ever driven or picked up by parents. The Center, I surmised, was an important place in the lives of these youth. Not only did they eat dinner there, it provided them a place to do their homework and a forum for participation in clubs and sports leagues. Another striking feature at the Center was that besides the full-time staff of three, it was utilized exclusively by only two age groups of Canal Town residents: children from the bilingual school and senior citizens. Although some area high school teenagers would occasionally stop by, I learned by talking to them that when a certain age was reached, the Center was seen as "uncool" and mainly a place for little kids.[2] Senior citizens mostly visit the Center in the first part of the day, and then typically clear out as the steady stream of youth arrive from school. All the while during my volunteer work, only on a few occasions did I ever see a Canal Town parent visit the Center or walk/drive a child home.

My thoughts about these observations began to dovetail with questions about the use of public space that my advisor, Lois Weis, was grappling with at the time. As part of a research team of graduate students headed by Lois Weis and Michelle Fine, we were reading and talking about the use of space in urban communities in the postindustrial north. I talked with Lois at length about the Center—how I noticed only certain youth were in attendance, how activities such as Girls' Club and sports leagues seemed so important to these youth, and how I never saw parents stop by. With Lois's encouragement, I formulated a potential research question based upon how poor white middle school youth in a restructuring economy construct indentities in both formal and informal sites of education. Middle school youth are at a precarious age, given the fact that according to community trends, in the not so distant future, they will likely consider themselves too old to attend. As these youth currently spend most of their waking hours in the school and the Center, I wanted to push outside the boundaries of the school and explore interinstitutional linkages between these sites to see how they are simultaneously used in the construction of poor white adolescent gendered identities.

My first step was to schedule an appointment with Felicia, the white thirty-four-year-old director of the Center. I spoke to Felicia about my intentions to conduct observations and in-depth interviews with middle school girls, boys, and Center staff, and how I planned to observe these same youth in the school and interview their teachers. I had known Felicia for a while at this point, and was very comfortable going to her with this request. Although the entire staff were longtime residents of Canal

Town, Felicia was the only one who had gone on to college, eventually receiving a nursing degree from the local state college. Stating she was familiar with the difficulties of being a student, Felicia was more than amenable to my request.

My next hurdle was to gain access to the bilingual school. I made an appointment with the principal at the end of the school year prior to my intended entry the next fall. This was my first meeting with the principal, who was an African American woman who had only been at that school for a year and who was quite new to principalship in general. As I greeted the principal and briefly explained my project, she immediately put me at ease. Although I had to submit a fomal request to City Hall in order to conduct research in urban public schools, the principal said she would help my case in any way she could. She called City Hall in an effort to endorse my work. Conveniently, the principal also sent a letter to all of the sixth, seventh, and eighth grade teachers, asking them if they would mind my presence in their classes, hallways, and so forth, and if they would be willing to be interviewed. One week later, the principal called me at home to report that no one objected. I then visited all twelve teachers in the mornings before classes in order to further familiarize them with my research and to set up an observation and interview schedule.

Having secured official access, I was now able to begin my fieldwork. I would go to the school each day, and then walk over to the Center, alternating travel with different groups of youth. Upon arrival, I would begin my own observations. After about six months, I began interviewing. The research necessitated that I move to this city for the duration of the investigation.

DATA COLLECTION

In this project, methods of data collection include participant observation, in-depth interviews, and document analysis. These various ways of gathering data allow for the triangulation of findings and the convergence of themes in ways that are multidimensional (Bogden & Biklen, 1992). Entering the universe of urban poor white middle school girls and boys as a white female relatively young researcher was a daunting task. In the school, youth from the Center immediately treated me as a friend, while the other students seemingly viewed me as a new student teacher. Word soon got out among youth that I was involved with the Center. The youth from the Center seemed to flaunt this information, which likely, in the long run, weakened my relationship with those students who did not attend. At the Center, I was positioned in a number of complex, and often emotionally demanding ways, including friend, counselor, teacher, older sister, and mother.

Between three and four days each week, I visited the school and the Center, collecting data through observations in classrooms, in the halls, and in the cafeteria of the school; and in the kitchen, the indoor swimming pool, and the recreational area of the Center. Attention was paid to the organization of the building, activity areas, classrooms, and administration of the school and the Center. Although I was an already known figure at the Center, it was my constant concern at the school that I remain as unobtrusive an observer as possible, especially during the early months of fieldwork while I was becoming familiar with the culture of the institution, and as others were easing into a relationship with me. When I sat in classrooms, teachers sometimes asked my opinion about a point of instruction, which made me uneasy, as I was mainly interested in building trust among informants. A running record of activity and anecdotal information was handwritten on-site each day; later that evening, these observations were expanded into detailed sets of field notes in computer files.

In addition to participant observation, I also conducted in-depth tape-recorded interviews. In the school, I interviewed twelve sixth, seventh, and eighth grade teachers and the principal. These interviews were held in classrooms before or after classes. At the Center I interviewed eighteen white youth and three staff members. I also interviewed three former Canal Town residents, mostly in their homes. All interviews lasted between one-and-one-half to two hours. Many of the teacher interviews began before class, and then were continued during a free period. Those interviewed were reminded they could turn the tape recorder off at any time. Interviews with minors required that I receive guardian consent. Permission forms were issued to all the youth, and within one week, they were returned to me completed. In-depth interviewing allowed for the exploration of adolescents' perceptions of themselves and their schooling and Center experiences as well as the patterns that emerged during observation.

Documentation about the school, the Center, and the neighborhood in which both sites are located was gathered from historical and policy records and through oral histories of long-term residents. Documentation I collected includes mission statements and census tract data. Economic data from the area spanning close to a century were also gathered in order to analyze economic trends, which helped to locate the research in a particular time in a postindustrial economy. School and district records were additionally reviewed as they related to the creation of cultural forms in the school. Literature on programs and activities available at the Center was also examined.

With the purpose of gathering some background information on the Canal Town youth and participating teachers, I disseminated a short questionnaire seeking biographical and demographic information. As part of the questionnaire, I asked informants to describe their racial/ethnic/cultural heritage. From this question, I found that all of the Canal Town youth identify as white, while six teachers identify as white, six teachers identify as Puerto Rican, and the principal identifies as African American. Throughout this research, I identify individuals by race/ethnic/cultural heritage as they self-identify.

I was able to stick to my schedule of transcribing data as they were gathered. During the transcription process, I began to familiarize myself with the data through numerous readings and re-readings of the text. After the data were collected, I spent the entire summer reading the narratives and notes. Then, in order to make the data accessible, I began to break it down into small component parts, or codes. Next, I created computer files that corresponded to each code. By highlighting portions of coded text, it was copied and transferred into the appropriate file. The next step was to go through the interviews and field notes, coding all the data and copying sections of text into their respective code files. I also created file folders in which to organize documents I had coded. Once this was done, I sifted through the coded data for common themes that swirled around and across codes. Such analysis delves deeply into narrative, excavating spoken and hidden meanings that give individual voices a collective forum.

Observations, interviews, and documentation within and across both sites were combined to form a lens through which to view interinstitutional linkages in the cultural construction of poor white Canal Town adolescent identities. In this ethnography, identities are analyzed as produced in relation to school and Center forms, practices, and larger social structures. As the history of Canal Town reveals, the community and the structures within stand upon contested terrain in terms of the notion among white residents that "others are taking over." Likewise, in the data, the structural dimensions of the school and the Center were found to be sites of immense struggle across similar dimensions. The cultural production of gendered identities among urban poor white Canal Town youth positions and shapes the spaces inside the school and the Center for specific uses. As a critical ethnographer, by burrowing deeply into narrative lines and forms of meaning, I am able to stand on the edge of these spaces and peer inside.

YOUTH BACKGROUND

In order to obtain a systematic sense of who these eighteen poor white sixth, seventh, and eighth grade youth are, I share information collected during the individual interviews which pertains to the home life of these participants. Out of the nine girls—Anne, 11; Rosie, 11; Sally, 11; Erin, 12; Elizabeth, 12; Lisa, 12; Katie, 13; Christina, 13; Hannah, 13—only Erin says she lives with both parents. Elizabeth, Anne, and Katie maintain they live with their mother, siblings, and their mother's steady boyfriend. The rest of the girls—Christina, Hannah, Lisa, Rosie, and Sally—report they live with their mother, siblings, and, on occasion, their mother's different boyfriends. Besides Erin, Christina is the only one who says she is in contact with her biological father, while the remaining girls contend they have no knowledge of their father's whereabouts. In terms of employment, seven of the girls state their mothers are not presently working, nor have been in the past, except for Elizabeth, who says that her mother used to work as a secretary years ago. Of the adult men in the lives of these girls who contribute to household expenses, Erin tells that her father holds a part-time job in the trucking industry, while Katie is the only girl to claim her mother's boyfriend earns money for their family. As Katie explains, her father collects items on trash day which he sells to pawn shops. Erin says her family receives food stamps, while all of the other girls come from families that rely on food stamps and AFDC. Regarding housing, Erin lives in a home her parents inherited from her grandparents, while the rest of the white Canal Town girls live in apartments.

Out of the nine poor white boys who participated in this research—Peter, 11; James, 11; John, 11; Andrew, 12; Sam, 12; Robbie, 13; Chris, 13; Jack, 13; Randy, 13—Robbie and Jack report they live with both parents. Andrew, John, and Randy each state they live with their mother, siblings, and their mother's steady boyfriend; while Peter, Randy, and Sam contend they live with their mother, siblings, and their mother's different boyfriends. Chris says he lives with his father and siblings. Only Peter and Randy say they are in contact with their biological fathers, both of whom are currently incarcerated. With respect to jobs, all of the boys explain their mothers are presently unemployed, and have not worked in the past. Robbie states that his father has a seasonal job as a window installer, and Chris says his father works part-time pumping gas at a neighborhood gas station. The remaining boys remark that the adult men at home do not contribute to the family's income. All of the boys mention their families receive food stamps and AFDC. In terms of living quarters, the white Canal Town boys all live in rental property.[3] The majority of both these girls and boys claim the adults at home have marijuana, crack, and alcohol problems. Although I have witnessed some of this behavior myself, I have no way of testing the extent of this reality.

As the white youth of Canal Town narrate their family histories, it becomes clear that they, their siblings, and their parents are ensnared within the impoverished clutches of an inhospitable economy. It can also be said local family life was not always this way, as the youth have heard stories of a time during their grandparents' day, when things were different. Unlike the white working class high school students in Freeway (Weis, 1990), who watched their fathers work in heavy industry and then lose their jobs ten years later, the younger poor white Canal Town youth have never seen their fathers involved in stable employment. This is likely the case as industry was experiencing massive layoffs and shutdowns by the time their parents were going through high school in the 1970s and 1980s.[4] In piecing together remnants of family history, the youth recollect that their grandfathers once had good jobs.

> KATIE: I really don't know much about my father. I know he didn't ever have a job and he was real into drugs. . . . Before my grandfather died, like, he used to tell me that he had a really good job working at the steel mill. He did something with coils, I think.

> CHRISTINA: Basically my dad doesn't do anything . . . my granddad, though, he liked to work, unlike my dad. He worked scooping at Starks [grain elevator] from when he was a teenager to when he was, like, old. He even used to own a house, although he lost it when he stopped working. I always wish my dad liked to work like that.

> ERIN: My dad has a job; he drives a truck, but it's only when they [trucking company] need him. . . . My grandma told me my granddad had a great job, in a steel factory or someplace like that. . . . I live in the house, still, that he bought. . . . My grandma signed it over to my mother.

> CHRIS: My dad works at the gas station [in Canal Town]; actually he pumps gas . . . he really doesn't make much. . . . My grandfather used to work full-time though . . . he worked at _____ Steel [local steel plant]. He made, like, a lot. That's what he [grandfather] used to tell me. . . . I try to talk my dad into getting a good job like that.

> SAM: I never knew my father, and my mother's boyfriend sure as hell don't work ever. . . . My grandma, like, before she went senile, used to say my grandpa made really good money down in the steel mill . . . I guess his job was to melt the metal or something.

According to their narrations, the poor white Canal Town youth are a generation removed from firsthand experience with working class life. Living with adults who they report do not have stable jobs, and in most cases, any employment, these adolescents have learned from their grandparents that they have historical connections to heavy industry. According to Christina and Chris, their fathers do not have labor jobs because they are lazy or do not want such work. Missing among these youth is any sense that the industry which supported such jobs no longer exists, even though boarded-up factories are scattered throughout the neighborhood. These poor white girls and boys are not growing up with a steady family wage, and, instead, have been pushed with their parents into lives of poverty.

CHAPTER 3

Canal Town Girls

In this chapter, I focus on emerging female identity among the poor white Canal Town girls. Female identity among these girls surfaces in relation to that of the constructed white male and in respect to that of the male and female "other." In terms of the future, the white girls are envisioning lives in which, by charting a course of secondary education, they hope to procure jobs and self-sufficiency. However, as their narrations indicate, such plans are fueled with the hope that by living independent lives as single career women, they will bypass the domestic violence that rips through their lives and those of their mothers. As they position African American males and Puerto Rican males and females as inferior and on the margins of what is acceptable behavior, these white girls locate themselves at the center of Canal Town life, coded white and superior.[1] This exploration of white female meaning making evidences processes among individual girls that are, for the most part, quite similar. This can likely be attributed to the exclusivity of the peer culture and the fact that these females rarely travel outside the neighborhood.

During the past fifteen years, much work has been done on girls and women at school (Valli, 1988; Holland & Eisenhart, 1990; Weis, 1990; Raissiguier, 1994). Such ethnographic research has uncovered ways in which schools serve to reinforce a gender hierarchy whereby males are considered dominant as compared to females. By not challenging patriarchal dominance in the larger society, it has been argued that schools perpetuate such relations. Also explored in such studies is the formation of female youth cultures, and how these cultures are connected to broader structural inequalities (McRobbie, 1978; Smith, 1988). While all of this work is important in terms of understanding the ways in which institutions contribute to unequal outcomes for females, as well as the ways in which the cultures produced by girls and women contribute to these outcomes, the issue of violence as embedded in these arrangements remains unexplored.

Michelle Fine and Lois Weis have examined this theme as it boldly emerged in their data on the lives of poor and working class white adult women and the production of identity (1998). My studies have been informed by such work, and like these researchers, I did not set out to examine domestic violence in the lives of poor white girls. Knowing about such abuse, however, paved the way for me to listen carefully to this guarded secret. While it is widely argued that violence in the home appears across social classes, it is now generally understood there is more such abuse among poor and working class families. It has also been found that white working class women experience more abuse as compared to working class women from other cultural backgrounds, and are more apt to treat their abuse as a carefully guarded secret.[2]

Another aspect of the construction of white adolescent female identity that emerges in the poor white Canal Town girl data includes expressed racism toward those from culturally oppressed groups. This finding contradicts existing work, in which a component of only white male identity formation depended upon denigration of the racial "other" (Weis, 1990; Fine et al., 1997). In earlier studies on females, white working class girls primarily elaborate identities around immediate, but historically inscribed gender struggles (McRobbie 1978; Weis, 1990). Although the white Canal Town girls do not patrol racial borders to the extent of white males in the literature, they *do* narrate lives that are being compromised by what they believe to be the deviant actions of those of African and Puerto Rican descent. As I conducted these interviews in the neighborhood community center, I attribute the girls' open discussion about racist attitudes to the informal and predominantly white site in which they have come to make my acquaintance, and to the fact that they had known me for more than a year prior to being interviewed. Since as compared to the streets and the school, the Center is seen by these white girls as a sanctioned or safe space, they may feel they do not have to be guarded.

JOBS AND CAREERS

Similar to the white Freeway females (Weis, 1990), the Canal Town girls do not narrate a marginalized wage labor identity. Instead, for both groups of females, securing a job or a career is a central goal. As the white Canal Town girls are only in middle school, their plans for the future may not yet be as specific or thought-out as those of the Freeway high school juniors. The point is that when asked to describe what they want their lives to look like after high school, the white Canal Town girls stress going to college and/or obtaining a good job, and like the Freeway females, only mention marriage or family after being asked.

CHRISTINA: I want to be a doctor. . . . I'll have to go to college for a long time. . . . I don't know where I'll go [to college], hopefully around here. . . . I'm not sure what type of doctor, but I'm thinking of the kind that delivers babies.

HANNAH: I want to be a leader and not a follower. . . . I want to be a teacher in Canal Town because I never want to leave here. . . . I want to go to [local] community college, like my sister, learn about teaching little kids . . . I definitely want to be a teacher.

KATIE: I want to be a scientist; I just love math. . . . I want to stay [in Canal Town]. If I live someplace else I won't be comfortable. . . . I'm shy. . . . I want to work with, like, chemicals, test-tubes.

LISA: I probably see myself as an educated person with a good job. The one thing I hate to see myself as is to grow up being a drunk person or a homeless person on the streets. . . . I would like most of all to be an artist, you know, with my own studio. . . . I'm going to start with cosmetology when I go to _____ [local high school], and then take it from there.

ERIN: I'd like to go into carpentry. I already help my dad fix stuff, like the table . . . I just want to be a carpenter. I want to go to college and also be a carpenter which is something you don't got to go to school for; you just become one. . . . It's just what I want to be.

All of these young girls envision further education in their future, but most do not yet have a clear sense of which school they hope to attend or how long they plan to go.[3] Christina is the only one who talks about a career that absolutely requires a four-year degree and beyond, while it is uncertain whether Hannah, Katie, Lisa, or Erin might pursue their goals by obtaining a two- or four-year degree. Christina, Katie, and Erin intend "nontraditional" careers in male-dominant fields, while Lisa and Katie choose those which are typically female. Lisa seems the least committed to any career, and tells me she is encouraged by her guidance counselor to sign up for the female-dominated occupation, cosmetology, in high school. Due to their young ages, any of these girls may switch ideas about careers a number of times, yet when asked about the future, all of them focus their energies on the single pursuit of furthering their schooling and landing a job. Worth noting, Lisa says she worries about being homeless, which is likely a chronic fear among poor youth.

The white girls of Canal Town are the daughters of presently poor adults. The girls' grandparents, however, were part of the working class tradition of laborers in which the men brought home a family wage (Smith, 1987). The girls report that none of their parents continued their education beyond high school and a few did not graduate from grade twelve. College, these girls say, is not really an option that is discussed much at home. Perhaps Hannah has the clearest idea of where she would like to go to school because she is the only girl who I worked with that has an older sibling enrolled in an institution of higher education. Hannah's sister attends a nearby community college and studies interior design, a circumstance that likely influenced her little sister's plans. Interestingly, three of the females indicate that although they want to break out of cycles of dependence and have careers, they do not want to leave Canal Town—whether for school or work.

Although the importance of a job/career is emerging within poor white Canal Town girl identity, it cannot be determined whether these girls will follow through on their plans for further education/training. The outlook is not promising, as all but a few of their older siblings are negotiating lives riddled with substance abuse and early pregnancies, and conversations with the principal of the area high school reveal that very few local teenagers are enrolling in any form of advanced studies. Weis (1990) indicates that, based on an analysis of high school transcript dissemination by participants in her study, some of the white Freeway girls were sending their scholastic records to those schools which, to a certain extent, reflected their expressed desires for the future. However, an even larger number of these females did not apply to any institutions of higher learning, despite the centrality of job/career surfacing in their interviews.

Even though the Canal Town girls view education as important in obtaining their goals, to a certain extent, they both accept and reject academic culture and knowledge while in school. Similar to the white Freeway females (Weis, 1990), I observed that on a daily basis while in class, the white Canal Town girls copy homework, pass notes, and read magazines/books, or in other words, participate in the form rather than the content of schooling. In a small number of instances, these females also display resentment toward school authority. Weis delineates that the resentment exerted toward institutional authority as seen in previous ethnographies is typically male and is linked to the historical contestation between capital and workers. Because, historically, white women mostly labored in the private sphere or in a pool of marginalized wage labor, they did not directly engage in such struggles. Weis, therefore, explains it is not surprising that the white Freeway females did not exhibit expressed resentment. Although during the interviews at the Center, a few of the white Canal Town girls do evidence contempt for school authority, this resentment revolves around something completely different—the notion of racial privileging.

> ERIN: My Spanish teacher is racist. She lets the Puerto Ricans do whatever they want to do. And the white girls are just out of it. The white kids have to do all the work. Like when this one girl [Puerto Rican] would say, "I'm not taking Spanish," the teacher would be like, "Okay." And when I asked if I had to do an assignment she would say "yes." And then I would say, "What about her [Puerto Rican girl]?" and the teacher would say, "Oh, she doesn't have to do that work." I

told Ruby [white, elderly activities coordinator at the Center], and she went and talked to the teacher. Ruby has had to do this a couple of times the past couple of years or so.

KATIE: The teachers here like Puerto Ricans better than whites. . . . They [Puerto Ricans] get away with murder while we [white students] are made to do more work and are blamed when things go wrong.

Anger seemingly directed toward authority actually represents an overall emerging sense of racism among the white Canal Town girls. According to Erin and Katie, teachers favor the Puerto Rican students, while those who are white are given more work and are being unfairly blamed for problems within the school. That these girls view race as an issue around which to exhibit anger is a salient point, and will be elaborated upon later.

FAMILY

The Canal Town girls, like the older white working class females of Freeway (Weis, 1990), view jobs and careers as a central part of their futures, which is in vivid contrast to young women in previous studies (McRobbie, 1978; Valli, 1988; Rassiguier, 1994). But while the Freeway females mention the desire for marriage and family in their futures only after they financially secure themselves through education and entrance into the public world of paid work, with the exception of Lisa, most of the Canal Town girls contend they do not wish to have husbands, homes, and/or families at all. Rather, the Canal Town girls reveal they are looking to the life of a single career woman as a way to circumvent the abuse which they see inscribed in future families/relationships with men. In constructing identities, it quickly becomes clear that seeking refuge from domestic violence plays a big role. For many of these girls, the future includes avoiding marriage and family altogether and getting a job so they can rely upon themselves.

CHRISTINA: I don't want to be married because if I was married my husband would want a kid. I don't want to have a kid because its father may not treat us right . . . hitting and stuff. . . . There's not enough for everybody, and the kid shouldn't have to suffer. . . . I want to always stay in Canal Town . . . live alone. . . . At least I know trouble here when I see it.

HANNAH: I don't want to get married and be told to stay at home . . . and be someone's punching bag. . . . I'll get a one-bedroom apartment and live alone and just try to be the best teacher I can be.

KATIE: I can't see myself being with a guy because they don't know how to not hit . . . that's, like, why I don't want to be married or have, like, a kid. . . . I'm going to go to school and be something really good.

LISA: I guess I sort of want to be married, but I want to be free at the same time, and that's not going to happen. I won't be able to do what I want if I'm married. . . . He's got to treat me good and respect me for who I am and not for what he wants me to be, and not for what I did in the past . . . not a lot of hitting. . . . I just don't know if that exists. . . . I'd rather live by myself, focus on a career.

ELIZABETH: I don't know yet [if I want to marry]. With the problems that happen, you never know. A person can act nice before you marry them, and then after they can be mean to you. They have all the power. They can make us do everything. My uncle is as lazy as hell. He makes my mom go to the store all the time. He makes us walk. My mom likes it, but I hate it. . . . We don't have a car, but he gets cable and my mom pays for it. He makes my mom pay for all the bills. We get our clothes from other people, but he buys his new. . . . I don't know if it's fair to have kids. If you don't put your kids first, you shouldn't bring them into the world. . . . If I get married, it will be to someone who's intelligent, willing to help, someone who doesn't drink, and someone who isn't violent. . . . I don't think it exists, so I want to just get a good job and live alone.

The Freeway (Weis, 1990) females say they desire careers so they do not have to depend upon a demanding husband. They also say they want to be prepared in the event of divorce or a husband's job loss. The girls of Canal Town, however, articulate they are not simply devising career-oriented plans to escape a patriarchal-dominant home. Rather, these girls specifically say they view a job as the ticket to a life free of abuse. By concentrating energies on the world of work instead of family, some of the girls feel they can spare bringing children into the world, whom they feel often bear the brunt of the problems of adults. As Elizabeth resolves, "If I get married it will be to someone . . . who doesn't drink, and [to] someone who isn't violent. . . . I don't think it exists, so I want to just get a good job and live alone."

While the Canal Town girls say they want to live as independent women in the public sphere, they are effectively developing such identities in response to violent men. By dreaming of living single, self-sufficient lives in the hopes of sidestepping violence, as will be seen, these females are not holding males accountable for abusive behavior. Males and their symbolic and material dominance cannot simply be erased from life, particularly when goals are to enter the public world of paid work. At this point in time, with little contact with institutions of higher education and careers outside Canal Town, many of these girls envision themselves continuing to live inside this sometimes violent neighborhood in which they are being raised.

DOMESTIC VIOLENCE

In present research on the conditions of poor and working class white women's lives, Weis et al. (1997) make a distinction between "settled lives" women, who exist in what appear to be stable, intact family structures, and "hard living" women, who move from household to household, partake of public assistance when needed, have less education, and have more low paying employment.[4] Both groups of women, however, negotiate lives saturated with domestic violence, the only difference being that "hard living" women exit from their homes and make their troubles public. Weis et al. raise concerns about the futures of these females, as the guiding philosophy of the federal government is to cut public assistance, thereby pushing family members deeper into private spaces, many of which are unhealthy.[5]

Considering the findings of Weis et al. (1997), it is crucial to begin to understand what life is like for the daughters of such white females, some of whom often have no choice but to ride along these supposed cycles of abuse.[6] Among the Canal Town girls, eight out of the nine depict lives which can be described as "hard living," while only Erin lives a seemingly "settled" life. When these young girls are asked to describe their neighborhood, they soon begin to tell stories of women being abused at the hands of men.

> ERIN: It's a pretty good place to live. . . . There's lots of auto crashes, drunk people. Lots of people go to the bars on Friday and Saturday and get blasted. They're always messing with people. Some guy is always getting kicked out of the bar for fighting. Guys are mostly fighting with their girlfriends and are getting kicked out for punching so they continue to fight in the street; I see it from my bedroom window, only the girl mostly gets beat up really bad.

> CHRISTINA: There's lots of violence in this neighborhood. Like there's this couple that's always fighting. When the guy gets mad he hits her. It happens upstairs in their house. She's thrown the coffee pot at him and the toaster, they [coffeepot and toaster] landed in the street . . . I saw it while walking by. . . . The guy would show off all the time in front of his friends. One day when he was hitting her she just punched him back and told him she wasn't going to live with him anymore. He used to hit her hard. She used to cry but she would still go out with him. She said she loved him too much to dump him. A lot of people go back.

> HANNAH: It's overall a nice neighborhood. . . .There's like a lot of physical and mental abuse that goes on. Just lots of yelling. I know one mother that calls her daughter a slut. She tells her, "You're not worth anything; you're a slut." . . . There's one family where the mother's

boyfriend sexually abused her little girl, and stuff like that. The girl was like 7, and, like, he's still with them. The mother didn't care. . . . It's like fathers and boyfriends beat on the kids. They [mothers] don't take a stand. They don't say, "Well, you know that's my daughter" or "that's my son." It's like they don't care. They think that they're just to sit down and be home . . . they just sleep all day or watch TV. Some of them drink all day and are high and spend a lot of time sleeping it off.

ROSIE: My neighborhood's quiet sometimes. It's a nice neighborhood, I guess. Sometimes it could be violent. . . . Like there was my mom's friend who came over once with bruises all over. Her boyfriend beat her up because she had a guy from downstairs come up to her house. The boyfriend got real mad and he was going to kill her because he was jealous. I didn't see the fight but I saw her. She looked like a purple people eater. . . . There's this one girl who got beat by her boyfriend. She did drugs and had another boyfriend, and the first boyfriend found out and got jealous. Violence is pretty much common in people's lives. About 95 percent of the world is angry. They attack things or litter, abuse people, and do other bad things like rape or kill. It's just the way it is.

Even though the community is seen as "a pretty good place to live" and "overall a nice neighborhood," the girls' descriptions of residency quickly devolve into stories of violence—mostly violence directed toward women by men in both public and private spaces. As Erin—who lives across the street from a tavern—watches out the window from her second-story flat, it is a normal occurrence for men to hit women in public sites, such as in a bar or on the street. As Christina walks through her neighborhood, she observes that violence also exists between men and women behind the closed doors of homes. Christina also notes that women often return to their abusive partners. Hannah distinguishes between different types of abuse—physical and mental—and gives examples of abuse between mothers and boyfriends, daughters and sons.[7] Rosie, it can be argued, is so desensitized to abuse that she humorously recalls how a badly beaten friend of her mother resembled a "purple people eater." In Rosie's view, "about 95 percent of the world is angry. . . . It's just the way it is."

Although these girls may look at abuse differently, they all are quick to recognize violence as a defining feature of their community. Missing in these perspectives, however, is the recognition that men are accountable for their abusive behavior. Instead, some girls blame women for letting males hit them and for returning to violent relationships. It is as if they are of the opinion that it is acceptable or normal for males to abuse females, and that it is the women's duty to negotiate their way around this violence. Hannah, for instance, is very critical of many neighborhood mothers who she feels are not putting their children's needs first. The data also indicate that violence is not necessarily hidden or kept a secret in Canal Town. Rather, despite their young ages, these white girls have heard of abuse in a variety of contexts and forms, and, according to their narrations, females in this community do not always endure their violence in isolation. Rosie, for example, reveals that a neighborhood woman sought refuge with her mother after a severe beating.

For these females, abuse does not just exist in public places and in the private dwellings of others. Violence also occurs in their own homes. Similar to poor and working class adult white women (Weis et al., 1997), in talking about personal experiences with abuse, the white girls typically contextualize violence as part of the past, as "things are better now." The younger females, though, are not as consistent in packaging such events in history. For instance, Elizabeth and Sally shift from present to past in describing the abuse in their homes. Many white Canal Town girls recall chilling vignettes of unbridled rage that pattern their upbringing.

ELIZABETH: I want my mother's boyfriend to stop drinking so much. He drinks a lot. Like a sink full of beer cans, because his friends come over a lot too. They bring over cases and he usually gets drunk off a 12-pack. . . . Like every other day he will start screaming and blaming things on my sister, me, and my mom. My mom tells him, "No, it's not our fault." He forgets a lot too, like what he did with his money, or where he puts his pens and pencils. He starts screaming at us because he thinks we take them. The house has to be a certain way. If one thing is out of place, he'll hit us or lock us in the closet for a while, until my mom screams so much he lets us out . . . but things are better now.

SALLY: I used to think of myself as a zero, like I was nothing. I was stupid; I couldn't do anything. . . . I don't anymore, because we're all done with the violence in my house . . . I've tried to keep it out since I was a kid. . . . My mom and John [mother's boyfriend] will argue over the littlest things. My mom is someone who is a violent person too. Sometimes she hits us, or he does. Then she would take a shower and we would get all dressed up, and we would all go out somewhere. After something bad would happen, she would try to make it better. She's a real fun person. . . .We're really close. We make cookies together and breakfast together.

ANNE: My mom and her boyfriend constantly fight because they drink. When I was little I remember being in my bed. I was sleeping, only my other sisters came and woke me up because my mom and her boyfriend were fighting. We [Anne and sisters] started crying. I was screaming. My sisters were trying to calm me down. Our door was above the staircase and you could see the front door. I just had visions of me running out the door to get help because I was so scared. My oldest sister was like 9 or 10, and I had to go the bathroom and we only have one and it was downstairs. She sneaked me downstairs and into the kitchen and there was glasses smashed all over, there were plants under water, the phone cord was under water in the kitchen sink. It was just a wreck everywhere. But most of all, there were streams of blood mixing in with the water, on the floor, on the walls.

ROSIE: I remember one Christmas my mom and my uncle were fighting. I escaped out the window to get help for my mom. We were living on the bottom floor at the time. I didn't have time to take a coat or mittens, I just grabbed my goldfish bowl . . . I think it was because I didn't want to ever go back there. I immediately ran to the Center but it was closed, being like three in the morning or something. So I just ran around the neighborhood and water was splashing out of my goldfish bowl, and the fish were dying, and I was freezing, and I couldn't even scream anymore.

As these narrations indicate, domestic violence patterns the lives of these young poor girls.[8] In a moment of desperation Rosie seeks refuge at the Center, but it has long closed for the night. Mom can offer little salvation as she is often drunk, violent herself, or powerless as the man in her life is on an abusive rampage. As they escape into the icy night or are locked in closets, these girls have little recourse from the extreme and terrifying conditions which govern their lives. In Sally's case, her mother is also violent, yet is thought of as making up for that abuse by involving her daughter in family-style activities. Sally learns, therefore, not to see or feel pain. Given these accounts, it is easy to conclude that the effects of domestic violence are not something that can be contained at home, and the data indicate that exposure to abuse profoundly shapes the girls' behavior in other places, such as school.

ELIZABETH: About twice a month they [mom and boyfriend] fight. But not that far apart. Last time he [boyfriend] smacked me, I had a red hand on my face. I walked around with a red hand on my face, only I wouldn't let anybody see it. . . . I skipped school and the Center for, like, three days so no one would ask me about it . . . I hid in my closet until you could barely see it. Then when I went back to school, I stayed real quiet because I didn't want people to look at me, notice the hand on my face.

CHRISTINA: When I had a boyfriend he [father] got so mad at me. He told me I wasn't allowed to have a boyfriend. I didn't know that because he never told me. He said that if he ever saw him again I would get my ass kicked. So one day he heard that Robbie [boyfriend] walked me to school. Well, he [father] came over that night and pulled down my pants and whipped me with his belt. I was bloody and the next day full of bruises. But I hurt more from being embarrassed to have my pants pulled down at my age. It hurt to sit all day long at school; that's all I could concentrate on. I couldn't go to the nurse because then she would find out. Nobody knew how I hurt under my clothes. I couldn't go to gym because people would find out, so I skipped. I hid in the bathroom but got picked up by the hall monitor who accused me of skipping gym to smoke. I just got so mad when I heard this, I pushed her [monitor] away from me and yelled. I was out of control with anger when they were dragging me down to the principal's. I got suspended for a week and had to talk to a school psychologist for two weeks about how bad smoking is for your health.

ROSIE: My mom got money from her boyfriend for my school pictures, and when they came back, he saw them as I was getting ready for school . . . he threw them and said that I messed up my hair. But I got up an hour early that day to fix it, I remember, only my hair just flattened, not on purpose. He got real mad and picked up a lamp and threw it at her and it hit her but I tried to block it and got hit too. It fell on the floor all in pieces. She was crying because she was hurt and because he left and I was crying becauseI knew she would let him come back. So we were both crying, picking up the glass. Then I walked to school and I didn't open up my mouth onceall day because I thought I would cry if I did.

ANNE: Sometimes at school I just avoid teachers because they might feel sorry for me because they might see, like, bruises or something. . . . Sometimes I act bad so they won't feel sorry for me, then if they see a bruise or something they would think I deserved it. I would rather have them think that than getting the principal or nurse.

These glimpses into the lives of the Canal Town girls indicate that children from violent homes are learning at very young ages how to negotiate lives that are enmeshed in a web of overwhelming circumstances. Elizabeth talks about how her mother's boyfriend blames her and her mother and sister for all that is wrong, while Rosie gets hit with a lamp while trying to protect her mother. As they devise ways to conceal their bruises, they each face their pain alone. Elizabeth skips school and seeks shelter from the world in the same closet in which she is punished by her mother's boyfriend. Christina is choked on her anger and pain and separates herself from school activity only to become embroiled in another set of problems. As Rosie quietly sits through class, her physical and mental pain renders her completely disengaged from academic and social life at school. Anne deliberately acts bad to distract teachers from focusing on her scars of abuse.

In their analysis of domestic violence in the lives of poor and working class white women and the potential effects such abuse may have on
their children, Weis and Fine (1996) review a substantial body of mostly
quantitative literature in which such dimensions are explored. The narrations of the white Canal Town girls reflect findings in much of the
existing research. As these girls evidence, abuse at home makes it difficult to concentrate in school, and the hurt, anger, and fear that they harbor inside often renders them silent, which also corroborates other studies (Elkind, 1984; Jaffe, Wolf, & Wilson, 1990). According to Afulayan
(1993), some children blame themselves for the abuse, and skip school
to protect a parent from the abuser, while other children become ill from
worry. Depression, sleep disturbances, suicidal tendencies, and low self-
esteem are other symptoms exhibited by children living in violent homes
(Reid, Kavanaugh & Baldwin, 1987; Hughes, 1988).

All of the Canal Town girls reveal they spend incredible energy on
keeping their abuse a secret while in school. This "culture of concealment" is likely in response to a number of fears, including fear of public embarrassment, fear of further angering an abuser, and/or fear that
families will be torn apart by authorities. While observing the females at
school, I noticed that, on a few occasions, some of the girls sustained
bruises that perhaps could not be so easily hidden under long sleeves and
turtlenecks. One day, for example, Christina came to school wearing an
excessive amount of eye makeup, which was noticeable, considering she
usually did not wear any. While talking to her outside after school, I
realized that this was probably an attempt to conceal a black eye, which
could clearly be seen in the harsh light of day.

Interestingly, I did not hear any talk of domestic violence at school—
critical or otherwise. This finding parallels the poor and working class
white women in the study of Weis et al. (1997) who also were silent about
the abuse in their lives, which was similarly not interrupted by schools, the
legal system, and so forth. While at school, it did not seem to me that any
of the girls sought help from their white female peers, teachers, or anyone
else in coping with abuse. Instead, in the space of the school, a code of
silence surrounding domestic violence prevailed, even though the white
girls articulate an awareness of others' abuse throughout Canal Town.
Not once did I hear students or teachers query others about violence or
raise concern, nor was abuse even mentioned as a social problem in classes
in which human behavior was discussed. Even on the day that Christina
came to school attempting to camouflage a bruised eye, I did not observe
a teacher pull her aside to talk, nor did I hear her friends ask her if she was
alright. Dragged by their families from one violent situation to the next, it
is remarkable that these girls are, for the most part, able to get through
the school day, go home, and come back again "tomorrow."

RACE

Unlike the white working class girls of earlier studies (McRobbie, 1978; Weis, 1990), poor white Canal Town girl identity boldly emerges in relation to both that of the constructed white male and that of the constructed African American and Puerto Rican male and female. Although they do not focus so much on patrolling racial borders,[9] these girls dialectically elaborate a sense of self in their neighborhood, Center, and school with those of African and Puerto Rican descent in ways that begin to resemble white working class males (Willis, 1977; Weis, 1990; Fine et al., 1997). In such a way, these girls narrate highly individualized stories about how the quality of their lives is being compromised by the deviant actions of those from culturally oppressed groups. This research indicates that these poor white girls—who are a generation removed from working class life—*are* participating in systems of racism, although *differently* than white working class boys, due to the gendered nature of men's and women's roles with respect to work and home life, which today is being filtered through the effects of a restructuring economy. By looking at how racism gets played out through dimensions of gender, the expressions on the part of white females are also clearly seen as reflecting the dominant structure. When asked to describe changes in Canal Town over the past few years, the responses of the girls are threaded with racist sentiments which circumscribe the neighborhood and the Center.

> HANNAH: There used to be a Hispanic church here [in Canal Town], but people took exception; they forced it to close down. . . . The teenagers . . . between the ages of 10 and 16 . . . they broke the windows; they would scream together through the front door while Mass was going on, "Spics are gonna die." Then they spraypainted that on the side of the church and it closed down. . . . It's just that some Puerto Ricans are into serious trouble . . . not all are bad though.

> ELIZABETH: My uncle don't like Blacks because he got shot with a BB gun by one. He says if he ever sees a Black guy near me, he'll kill him. . . . They're [African American boys] always after me and my friends . . . we've got to be careful. . . . They should just stay in the projects.

> KATIE: There's been Puerto Ricans moving in [neighborhood], and when they did, white people started moving out. I guess they think the Puerto Ricans are going to start to bring violence into our neighborhood, all of which is true. . . . I heard all the Black kids carry guns, and if more Black people move in they will bring more drugs. . . . Most [people of African descent] live in the projects though.

ROSIE: Like if someone said something to me, like a Black kid, I would run home and tell my mom . . . we would just call the cops. This one time they [African American boys] came and did stuff to my sisters. They came to kick us and throw stuff at us. They started saying we were whores. . . . It was right by our house. My mother has this talking camera that she got for racial stuff and she recorded the incident and said what was going on because cops tend to not believe white people. Everyone gives special treatment to minorities. I have a few who are friends, but many are just bad.

SALLY: The Blacks and Puerto Ricans are trying to come in [neighborhood], a lot are dangerous; some have guns and drugs. Some [people of African descent] use whites to show off. Actually I'm against whites going out with Blacks, but I'm not prejudiced. When I was younger, Mario [African American boy] wanted to go out with me and I didn't want to. I told him I wasn't prejudiced, but I didn't want whites to go out with Blacks. . . . My uncle threatened to beat him if he [Mario] touched me.

These girls indicate that racist sentiments flow through Canal Town. Although a few mention having "a friend" from a culturally oppressed group, by and large, in homes and on the streets, those of African and Puerto Rican descent are thought of as criminal-like, carrying drugs and guns. According to the white Canal Town girls, these individuals are forcing their way into the community and are bringing in violence. Hannah reveals that area youth participate in forms of "community maintenance"; for example, she recounts how some white adolescents vandalized a Puerto Rican church and harassed parishioners during Mass to such an extent that the congregation closed down. Similar to the older Canal Town residents interviewed earlier, these white girls talk of crime and violence as something being "brought in" by those from culturally oppressed groups. The Canal Town elders revealed, however, that such activity was part of the Irish American history of the area.

As with earlier studies, males of African descent are thought of as being sexually menacing (Weis, 1990). Elizabeth says if her uncle sees an African American male near her, "he'll kill him." Rosie describes a scenario in which she and her sisters were seemingly harassed by a group of African American boys. She tells how she ran home to tell her mother, who, it appears, tried to capture what she believes are truant actions specific to those of African descent on a camcorder. Not only does Rosie feel "minorities" are given "special treatment," she relays it is vital for her mother to keep her daughters "pure" from an African American male presence.

Ironically, as the previous narrations of the Canal Town girls indicate, *white males*, in fact, are the ones who are responsible for actual violence in their lives. As the data reveal, these girls, however, point to African American boys as potential perpetrators. It seems white male abuse has become normalized and silenced to such an extent in the lives of these white girls that there is presently no critique. Being unable to recognize those who really threaten their safety, as they construct identities, these white females find someone to blame for their sense of violation in historically available scapegoats. This act of idealizing that which is white and female can be seen as linked to Carby's (1982) description of the ideology of the "cult of true womanhood." This cult, to which only white women can belong, explains Carby, has historically depended upon the stereotype of the sexually permissive Black woman and the sexually menacing Black man. By ascribing to this ideology, the white Canal Town girls arguably position white males—who are their actual potential abusers—as their protectors, thus further participating in their own victimization. Elizabeth and Sally, for instance, both indicate that white men in their families are involved in policing them from an African American male presence.

Personal accounts of how those from culturally oppressed groups are "less than" whites is a continuing theme in the white Canal Town girl data. In explaining how different youth get along at the Center, the white females position "others" at the margins, framing whiteness as normative.

> HANNAH: The Puerto Rican girls who come to the Center are okay. I'm glad no others come. No Blacks come, Blacks can be like dirty, mean, troublesome. I don't like the Puerto Ricans at school that seem Black. . . . My friend Marita [Puerto Rican] at the Center is almost my color.

> ROSIE: The Puerto Rican kids that I know at the Center get along with everyone. . . . They're way different than the Puerto Ricans at school . . . the ones there are like, they're like Black. Sometimes you can't tell the Puerto Ricans from the Blacks in the way they look. We get along [at Center]. In our school we don't get along because they just hate us, I guess [Blacks, Puerto Ricans]. And we hate them too. They [Puerto Ricans] should just talk English . . . the Puerto Ricans here [at Center] talk English. We know them here.

> ERIN: Black kids don't come to the Center because they don't like the white kids. . . . In school we have too many Puerto Ricans. There was a big fight in the lunchroom. The fight was with me and this boy Melvin. He don't like white at all. He's prejudiced. He's Puerto Rican. I asked him why he has a problem with whites. Then all the Puerto Rican girls screamed to me, "Why do you have a problem with Puerto Ricans?" I said, "I don't have a problem with Puerto Ricans." . . . Some of them you can't tell Black from white. Then I got in a fight with this

one girl named Vanessa [African American student] over Black and white [relations between those who are white and African American]. . . . She punched me in the face . . . I just went right off on her. I wasn't going to take this. . . . Whites are like, treated unfairly at school, and then we [Black, Puerto Rican, and white students] don't get along. At the Center we all get along.

CHRISTINA: In the early years of slavery, whites didn't like Blacks and Blacks didn't like whites. I'm way against that. I'm kind of prejudiced with mating, when a Black mates with a white. Because with animals, a squirrel can't mate with a cat. But they could still be friends. . . . Whites should be with whites, and Blacks should be with Blacks. At the Center it's mostly white and a couple of real shy Puerto Rican girls.

In this study, the white Canal Town girls overtly script those of African and Puerto Rican descent as "other," while making distinctions among "types" of Puerto Ricans. Taking part in the European constructed hierarchy of racial categories as described by Ani (1994), these females narrate an essentialized pyramid of those who are thought to be subpar as compared to their white selves. In this model, those who are white are the most worthy and thus occupy the top of the pyramid. Those of Puerto Rican descent come far below those who are white and exist in seemingly split categories—those who "seem" more African and those who "seem" more European. As Hannah, Rosie, and Christina indicate, they do not care for those Puerto Ricans that "seem Black." They also do not like it when you "can't tell Blacks from Puerto Ricans." Christina is vehemently opposed to interracial dating. As she makes the analogy that a "squirrel can't mate with a cat," Christina sees essentialized differences between those who are white and those who are of African descent, setting up Blacks as "other." Hannah and Erin acknowledge that the Puerto Ricans they do like have lighter skin and also speak English at the Center. Those who appear "Black" seemingly stand at the base of the pyramid.

Unlike at school, Erin and Rosie contend white and Puerto Rican youth get along at the Center. However, this may be the case because those who enter can be regulated by whites—the historical gatekeepers of the neighborhood. Only a small number of Puerto Rican girls actually attend. During my fieldwork, in only a few rare instances did I see a Puerto Rican boy or African American youth at the Center. Those adolescents from culturally oppressed groups who are most favored are arguably let through the door. As the white Canal Town girls script males of African and Puerto Rican descent as criminal-like and menacing, and as they do not care for Puerto Rican girls who "seem Black," they are arguably content that only a certain few Puerto Rican girls come to the Center. But even these Puerto Rican girls are not fully accepted into the white girl group. As the only community center in a multiethnic neighborhood that is staffed by white adults and is patronized by mostly white youth, race management often exists in raw forms.[10]

On a few occasions at the Center, I overheard some of the white Canal Town girls refer to the Puerto Rican Canal Town girls as "niggers." The white girls never directly called them this to their face, preferring the more discrete practice of uttering derogatory references in hushed tones among the confines of their white female peer group. One afternoon, for instance, Rosie, Christina, Elizabeth, and Katie were cleaning the gerbil cage. Marita and Lourdes—11-year-old Puerto Rican girls who are regular visitors to the Center—were walking by on their way to the food pantry to get a snack, when Tammy quietly joked, "I heard them niggers eat gerbils," a comment directed toward the two Puerto Rican girls, and followed by laughter from the group. Over the course of my observations, I never heard the white girls use racist terminology during supervised recreation.

The association of Puerto Ricans with those of African descent is not unusual among those of the dominant culture. In a recent study, in which the struggle among poor Puerto Rican men to carve out identities in economically depressed cities on the mainland is explored (Weis, Centrie, Valentin-Juarbe, & Fine, 1997), it is found that upon arrival in the States, these males enter a static white/Black way of viewing the world, comprised of European Americans on one end and African Americans on the other. While there is also a biracial structure in Puerto Rico, the authors argue it is possible there for those in the "middle" to move from one racial designation to the other, for instance, by raising their class status or through education levels. Even members of one family, explain the authors, can be identified via a number of different racial categories. When coming to the mainland, the Puerto Rican men in this research found the potential to fluidly move through the racial structure was replaced by a rigid, binary structure, and that they were being labeled "Black." These men strongly resist this racial labeling, and struggle to assert themselves as Puerto Rican.

The authors state there is racism in Puerto Rico and on the mainland toward those who are thought to be most "Black." The distancing on behalf of the Puerto Rican males interviewed from being considered "Black" is likely motivated, in part, by racism toward Africans.[11] In the case of Canal Town, in equating Puerto Ricans with those of African descent, the white girls are seemingly participating in the white/Black dichotomy, and with few exceptions, in their assessment, most Puerto Rican youth do not come close enough to the acceptable "white" end of the scale. As no Puerto Rican boys are in attendance at the Center, the data indicate they are being equated with Black males, and therefore, ladened with similar derogatory stereotypes.

The Canal Town girls made negative connections between those of Puerto Rican and African descent many times at the Center, which calls to mind a conversation that Simone—a 28-year-old white friend—told me she had with Marita.[12] Simone said she was commenting that when she was young, she went to Puerto Rico and found she could easily get by with just knowing English. Marita was responding that a lot of people in Puerto Rico speak English, when Allison, a white 7-year-old girl who was eavesdropping on the conversation had a puzzled look on her face and interrupted by asking Simone, "Are you Black or white?" Marita later told Simone that Allison and a lot of people think everybody in Puerto Rico is Black, and white people are not allowed inside. In this instance, again, Allison correlates Puerto Ricans with those of African descent.

In describing how students interact at the bilingual school, the white Canal Town girls evidence a sustained sense of racism. During the 1995–96 academic year, the total student population was 466. Of these students, 43 percent were white, 54 percent were Puerto Rican, and 3 percent were African American. Students of African descent from the bordering Pepper Projects were in attendance at another public school.[13] The white Canal Town girls position their white selves as the victims of "minority favoritism." From their perspective, students of African and Puerto Rican descent are acting "hard" and vying to be the school "tough guys," and the Puerto Rican teachers unfairly favor Puerto Rican youth.

SALLY: At school, all the Puerto Rican kids hang with the Puerto Rican kids, and all the white kids hang with the white kids; the Black hang with the Black. . . . In school the Blacks and the Puerto Ricans try to act hard and gang up on each other. . . . We [white Canal Town girls] go to Ruby if we have a problem, never our teachers because they favor the Puerto Ricans. The Puerto Rican teachers all live on the east side, in the Puerto Rican section. The Puerto Ricans who come here [to school] do too. I heard that some of them [Puerto Rican kids] are friends with their teachers outside of school. I heard that some of them [teachers and students of Puerto Rican descent] live on the same street.

ANNE: I kind of don't like all the races that are there [school]. The Puerto Ricans start with us. Like yesterday this Puerto Rican girl said to me, "You smell like fish," and that just got me so mad. I started crying. I told my friend Jane that's pregnant and she was going to beat them up. I told her not to because she's pregnant. She wanted to know who was messing with me, but I told her to calm down or she would lose her kid. . . . They [Black and Puerto Rican students] want attention and they want to be the school tough guys. The Blacks compete with the Puerto Ricans, the Puerto Ricans compete with the Blacks, and the white ones get blamed for all the trouble.

ERIN: Not all minorities are bad. I like a couple of the Puerto Rican girls at the Center, like, Marita, she's not bad. Sometimes, though, it seems like they [Puerto Rican students] are favored. I mean, they're the ones who are always getting into trouble. I mean, like just this past month, there were five fights in the halls. They [the fights] were all Puerto Rican versus Puerto Rican. So because of this they [principal, teachers] go and cancel the school skating party. So we [white youth] suffer.

KATIE: There's some really good Puerto Ricans at the Center. They come to the Center and don't expect special treatment. The minorities at school though, they get treated special. I mean that, like, because a lot of teachers are from the east side and so are the kids [students]. They laugh and joke about Spanish things [things having to do with Puerto Rican culture] and leave us [white friends] out. It's like the Puerto Rican teachers favor the Puerto Rican kids.

It is significant that these poor white girls attribute so much trouble to students of African descent, as they comprise an extremely small number at this school. The contempt held for these few students, and the conflation of those who are Puerto Rican with those of African descent, again, is likely linked to larger feelings of racism toward anyone or anything African. As Sally contends, and according to my observations, in school, youth group themselves according to race, particularly in the lunchroom and in classes in which there is no seating chart. Although some of the white Canal Town girls say they like the few local Puerto Rican girls who visit the Center, I did not witness them include them in their group of white friends from the neighborhood at school. Upset over "all the races," Anne mixes anger toward Puerto Ricans with those of African descent.

While both students of African and Puerto Rican descent are disliked by the white Canal Town girls at school, they exert the most concentrated anger toward Puerto Rican youth, who, as Sally, Erin, and Katie say, are given preferential treatment by teachers. Many of the Canal Town girls seemingly take exception to the sense of familiarity between some of the Puerto Rican students and teachers, who in many cases, come from the same neighborhoods on the east side. Because of her cultural reference point, Katie is resentful in that she feels she is being excluded from conversations in Spanish in which teachers and students of Puerto Rican descent allegedly talk and joke about things she knows nothing about. Another point around which white Canal Town girls express anger is having to take Spanish.

ROSIE: I'd rather learn French . . . I just hate it [Spanish]. I'm forced to learn something I don't understand and I don't want to learn. I know a lot of people who are mad about it. One advantage of learning Spanish is that when the Puerto Rican girls talk about you and think you don't know what they're talking about, you understand it and they don't even know it. They [administrators] should get rid of it. . . . Last time I looked, we spoke English in America.

ANNE: They [teachers, administrators] think we're going to need it [Spanish]. If someone comes to us speaking the Spanish language, why don't Spanish people stay in their own country and we stay in our country? They come to our country and people expect us to learn their language. We don't go to their country and expect them to learn our language, do we? No. So it should be like that.

SALLY: The girls [Puerto Ricans] talk about you in Spanish and you won't even know what they're saying. And you ask them what they're saying and they'll tell you, "Learn the language." It makes me mad. This girl in my class is always saying something in Spanish, and if I say "What?" and then I tell the teacher, she says, "If you don't know Spanish, it's your fault." If they're going to speak Spanish, they should tell someone who speaks Spanish and tell us in English. I told my mom about it and she said I didn't have to learn it. . . . She and her friends don't like it and she don't care if I learn it.

Particularly in school, the Canal Town girls position their white selves as the victims of "minority favoritism." Much expressed racism centers around the fact that they have to take Spanish as part of the bilingual school program, yet it is also linked to a larger sense of racism. Narrating a discourse of nativism, Rosie contends, "Last time I looked, we spoke English in America." Anne also complains, "why don't Spanish people stay in their own country and we stay in our country?" Sally says her mother does not care if she applies herself in Spanish class, suggesting that many other white people in the Canal Town community hold these sentiments.

The data indicate the Canal Town girls produce notions of identity around that of the constructed white male and those from culturally oppressed groups. Domestic violence, however, also emerges as a profound sphere in the shaping of white Canal Town girl identity. It is ironic that these girls view males of African descent as predators, as white males are the ones who actually pose the greatest threat to their safety on a daily basis. As the data powerfully unfold, these girls view violence in the home as normal. These girls also reveal that the school is not acknowledging the abuse in their lives, and therefore, encourages the "culture of concealment."

In the white spaces of the community center, the white Canal Town girls display racist attitudes that have been previously undisclosed in other studies (Valli, 1988; Holland & Eisenhart, 1990; Weis, 1990; Raissiguier, 1994). In this site, they elaborate identities based upon the racial "other," although at times, have a variegated understanding of race—for example, they speak of having a light-skinned Puerto Rican friend. As they talk about school, the white Canal Town girls animate unwavering anger toward those from culturally oppressed groups, due to their belief that "minorities" are being favored. In the final analysis, it seems the white girls collude their anger for Puerto Ricans and those of African descent, all of which is arguably based upon a deep racism for Africans. In this context, the Center seemingly stands as the only place where the white Canal Town girls feel safe from the violence which surrounds their lives, and where they can maintain a sense of whiteness and white privilege in juxtaposition to the racially diverse neighborhood and school.

CHAPTER 4

Canal Town Boys

In this chapter, I explore the construction of identity among the poor white Canal Town boys. I do not intend a direct comparison with the white females, instead considering only those aspects of identity that emerge the strongest in the data. Male identity among this group surfaces in a number of ways, including an expressed resentment toward school authority and in both sexist and racist attitudes. Struggles in the formation of identity among these boys often coalesce in the form of racial border patrolling. In producing a sense of self, their potential for directing violence toward the dialectically constructed "other" also emerges, which in their case, refers to white females and males from culturally oppressed groups.[1] Similar to white working class adult males (Fine et al., 1997), the stories of anger these boys narrate about those from culturally oppressed groups are told in a discourse of lost entitlement. Another aspect of young white male identity that will be a focus of this analysis includes an examination of conflicting ideas about education. Perhaps due, in part, to the tight-knit white male peer culture that is produced in the Center, and to the fact that these youth rarely venture outside their community, this exploration of meaning making reveals processes among individual boys that are strikingly similar.

Many ethnographic studies have been conducted in which the gendered experiences of boys and men at school are considered (Willis, 1977; Weis, 1990; Messner & Sabo, 1994; Connell, 1995). In various strands within this literature, researchers consider the construction of white women and those from culturally oppressed groups as "other." With the absence of labor jobs around which white working class men partially formulate a sense of manhood, Weis (1990) examines how Freeway high school juniors envision future patriarchal dominant households. In another example, by drawing attention to the multiplicity of masculinities among males, Connell (1995) explores how compulsory heterosexuality becomes a formidable context around which white working class subjectivities are produced. Researchers who examine male-only spaces in schools for white working class and middle class men indicate they often become intense sites for the development of negative attitudes toward white women and gay men (Messner & Sabo,

1990, 1994; Connell, 1993; Klein, 1993; Polk, 1994). While all of this work is important in terms of understanding the ways in which institutions contribute to the formation of masculinities, the issue of male violence against women remains relatively unexplored.

As previously discussed, adult poor and working class white women in a current study (Weis et al., 1997) are found to endure significant amounts of abuse at the hands of white men. Interestingly, although the poor and working class white males who were also interviewed as a part of the research say they are angry at women for taking their jobs, these males do not mention domestic violence at all. This is startling, considering these men were from exactly the same communities and have, therefore, also likely witnessed violence.[2] Aware of this discrepancy, and then hearing the Canal Town girls' narrations of abuse, I was prompted to ask carefully and then listen to what the white boys had to say.

Similar to white males in other studies (Willis, 1977; Weis, 1990; Fine et al., 1997), poor white Canal Town boy identity emerges in relation to expressed racism toward, in particular, their male peers of African and Puerto Rican descent. The slightly older white Freeway males co-produce African American male identity with their own, constructing African American males as a threat to white females, thus scripting their own role as protector (Weis, 1990). Poor and working class adult white males position the world of work and affirmative action and welfare programs as sites in which to script themselves as morally superior as compared to others (Fine et al., 1997). These highly individualized stories of anger as narrated by white males in both these studies—from teenage years to adulthood—are told without any reference at all to the larger eroding economy. The Canal Town boys also partake in a racially inscribed discourse over their assumed role as "protector" *and* in relation to what they consider to be the unfair funding of "minority" projects and programs in their community, school, and Center. These boys interpret funded programs to be at the expense of those who are white. Never critiquing their own economic dislocations, these boys seemingly view their impoverished lives as normal.

SCHOOL AUTHORITY AND MEANINGS

Earlier investigations of white working class masculine identity formation indicate that an oppositional stance is often taken in relation to school authority and culture. This "us versus them" attitude is rooted in historical contestations between capital and labor. Willis's (1977) "lads," for example, exhibit behavior that suggests resentment that balances on the edge of actual confrontation. By skipping school to have a "laff," the lads reject the abstract and individualistic nature of academics in favor of their peer group. By creating a culture in which they reject schoolwork, Willis contends the lads are wrestling to win symbolic and physical space from the school. Other studies of white working class school-aged masculine identity formation reveal similar ways in which academic content and culture is rejected (London, 1978; Everhart, 1983). A common theme in such ethnographic work is an attempt by white working class males to reject the mental labor of academics, and instead, to forge spaces in the school in which they can animate their own meanings.

The Canal Town boys also express resentment toward the institutional regulation of time and space while at school, and in some instances, this, too, can be seen as one stroke away from outright confrontation. Again, as Weis (1990) reminds us, such attitudes are historically inscribed in the working class *male* struggle between capital and labor. Not traditionally a part of that public sphere, the Canal Town girls do not evidence a resentment of authority nearly as much, and the anger they do voice is more reflective of their emerging sense of racism.[3] In detailing what they do and do not like about school, most of the boys exhibit disdain toward those who are viewed as in charge.

> ANDREW: There's no place to go in this school where they won't hunt you down, they don't give you any breaks. I mean, if you go to the bathroom between classes, you're gonna be late . . . so you get detention. It's like they [teachers/administrators] want to get you in trouble, get tons of us [students] in detention. . . . I don't like it [school] because of my teacher. . . . She hates me. I ask her a question and she starts yelling at me. . . . It's all about control with them . . . they got to know where you are and what you're doing at all times; like they have no trust whatsoever . . . they treat us like the elementary kids.

> CHRIS: The teachers, no matter what you do, even if it's an accident, they always yell and they try and get you suspended. They're always looking to get you in trouble. . . . They pop up behind cars in the parking lot just as you're lighting a cigarette. They're not even there to teach; they just want a paycheck. They [teachers] even admitted it to me. . . . I always have a click in my tongue, and today in school I clicked my tongue on accident. She [the teacher] started yelling at me and sent me down to the office . . . and the principal was screaming at me and I missed the whole class.

> PETER: It's like they just wait for you to do something they think is wrong . . . walking up and down the rows of tables in the cafeteria. . . . They hand out detention slips around here like candy. . . . They [teachers, administrators] know that we've [friends] got them figured out, [we] can see through their bullshit, and that's why they crack down on us harder.

RANDY: Sometimes I talk in a loud voice. I can't help it; it's just the way I was born. I was born screaming at the top of my lungs. I really can't control it. So sometimes my teachers think I'm saying things that make people [other students] laugh real loudly, on, like, purpose. But like I said, it's nothing I can control. They [principal, teachers] gave me suspension a couple of times because of it, which put me behind in my work.

Throughout my observations at the bilingual school, classes seem to run smoothly. Student challenges toward authority include subtle gestures which, at most, slightly throw off the pace of daily academic activity. Such actions encompass hiding chalk, stopping up water fountains with bubblegum, and releasing a snake in the teachers' lounge, to more elaborate disruptions, such as starting fires in the bathrooms and pulling emergency alarms. Similar to the white high school males of Freeway (Weis, 1990), although there was a constant undercurrent of resentment toward authority from these boys during my observations, there were no episodes that disrupted the cycle of the day.

Also paralleling the Freeway boys (Weis, 1990), on one level, the poor white Canal Town boys do not completely reject academics as do the "lads" (Willis, 1977). Chris and Randy, for example, complain that when they get into trouble at school, they are often punished in ways which get them behind in their work. When asked about their futures, however, unlike the Freeway males (Weis, 1990), the white boys of Canal Town do not associate their plans for the future to the closing of plants and factories. This is likely linked to the fact that these young males are even further removed from the days of industry, and thus have come to view poverty as somehow normal. This may, in part, also be the case because the Canal Town boys are younger and not thinking as seriously about the future as high school juniors, as it is seemingly so far away. For now, in terms of the future, many of these boys have wistful dreams of becoming professional athletes, and/or do not have clear plans for college.

ROBBIE: I want to be a lot of things. I want to go to college and be a superstar in sports. I want to be a hockey player, a basketball player, a baseball player. I want to be a lot of things. I would rather play first and then coach. . . . I want to stay in Canal Town. . . . I'm going to be a superstar, be being spotted one day while I'm playing and then I'll get picked up in the draft. . . . I'm gonna have money to burn.

JOHN: I want to be a basketball player or a lawyer. . . . I want to go to Harvard . . . I want to go because it's the best school around and I want to be rich.

PETER: I want to be a cop in Canal Town. . . . I guess I will have to go to college, maybe to _____ [local community college] because they have criminology there.

SAM: I want to go to college and become a millionaire, maybe play in the NHL . . . drive a Mercedes around Canal Town. . . . I'm gonna go to college and make tons of money when I get out.

The vagueness and impracticality of some of the Canal Town boys' plans for the future is likely due to their youth. It is, indeed, typical for particularly young boys to hold steadfast to the dream of making it to the rank of professional athlete. Still, most of these young males foresee higher education in their future, but do not seem familiar with the types of skills and thinking that can be learned in college or how it all might translate in the current economy. College, in other words, is a way to "become a millionaire," "to be rich," and "drive a Mercedes." This notion of higher education as a high-end commodity may be due to the fact that the boys say none of their parents went to college, and therefore, they may not be familiar with the market value of an undergraduate degree. Only Peter has defined goals that are arguably grounded in a vocation that is working class. Peter wants to become a police officer, and when asked how he plans to achieve his objective, he mentions a local postsecondary two-year program geared toward that profession. Interestingly, not one of these boys express an interest in wage labor, and again, none contextualize their responses in a changing economy.

Although most of these boys resent school authority, they also adhere to an understanding of the importance of further schooling in their futures.[4] This valuing of school meanings and forms, however, is not necessarily acted upon while at the bilingual institution, where students regularly fall asleep, copy assignments, and cause disturbances. School forms and meanings are both accepted and rejected by the Canal Town boys at one and the same time, as they begin to view education as somehow important to their futures. While the "lads" (Willis, 1977) participate in a wholesale rejection of institutional authority and school forms and meanings, the Freeway males (Weis, 1990) reveal contradictory attitudes toward schooling which are in keeping with those of the Canal Town boys. Weis, in part, attributes this paradox among the Freeway males to their understanding that jobs in industry no longer exist, and their expressed desire not to have to struggle to make ends meet. The white Canal Town boys' generational connection to a felt sense of entitlement to labor jobs has arguably been disrupted by a restructuring economy. However, these boys completely ignore broader economic issues, which is surprising, considering the neighborhood is strewn with rusting warehouses and grain elevators. College, instead, is seen as a way to get rich.

Weis (1990) chronicles how despite the Freeway boys' affirmation of college, only about one-third of the junior class actually took the pre-SAT and only about one-third of the senior class took the SAT, which is a required examination for entrance to most four-year institutions. Among those students who did take these tests, scores were slightly less than average. Mindful that grades can be viewed as merely constructed, grade reports were not that high among Freeway students. Low SAT scores and low grades, asserts Weis, will not permit Freeway youth entrance into the comprehensive college sector. Similarly, the Canal Town boys achieve mostly average to low grades. Like the Freeway male high school students, Sam, Robbie, and Jack have a tendency to settle for marks that are "passing."

> SAM: They [teachers, administrators] think they can control me, but as long as I pass I'll show them. . . . Last year when I passed they got so pissed. It was hysterical. . . . They did everything they could to hold me back, but I showed them, I passed! . . . They thought they had me by the tail . . . the joke's on them!

> *English, March 14, 1996*

> ROBBIE: [Robbie gets an essay back that he wrote on fishing] Hallelujah! I passed! Score: one for me, zero for them. . . . Maybe all those times being dragged to church finally paid off. . . . I'm getting my just dessert. . . . No one can hold back Robbie McGuire!

> *Last Day of School, June 20, 1996*

> JACK: I can't believe it, I passed! I got a 65.1! I'm gonna go to high school! I'm leaving this horse and pony show! . . . Got to celebrate tonight. [Runs to show friends his grade report. Congratulating, back slapping, high-fives. 65 is passing.]

Among many of the white Canal Town boys, there is an extreme sense of relief in just making it through. Satisfaction is gained by graduating to the next grade—even by the narrowest of margins. As Sam says, "they thought they had me by the tail," and as Jack likens his experiences as a student to a "horse and pony show," they use language that suggests triumph despite attempts by school authorities to control them or hold them back. Upon passing his English essay, Robbie clearly animates an "us versus them" attitude as he declares, "score: one for me, zero for them." Being content with achieving grades that are just passing, again, seemingly contradicts some of the white Canal Town boys' plans for the future, which include college followed by a lucrative career.

In many ways, it could be said the white Canal Town boys go through the motions of school. Besides the goal of just making it through, they are content to pass along the surface of learning, by copying homework and test answers from others—a practice that is more common among the oldest boys in this study.

Spanish, January 28, 1996

The teacher walks around checking homework. As she passes down one row, Robbie, who sits on the other side of the room, gets up to throw out some garbage. While doing this, he grabs the worksheet [homework] from a student who has been checked in, goes back to his seat, erases the name, and fills in his own. The teacher walks up Robbie's row and gives him a check for doing the homework. Robbie does this at least twice a week.

English, February 14, 1996

The homework assignment was to write a poem for Valentine's Day. Before the teacher gets to his row, Chris is scrambling to copy a poem from a card he received from another student. Another time, Chris gets a short story handed back graded an "A." Chris turns to me grinning and says he simply copied down the words to a Marylin Manson [alternative band] song. When I looked at his work I recognize the lyrics verbatim.

Math, March 3, 1996

In the hallway outside math class before a unit test on probability. Randy, Jack, Robbie, and some other white boys are huddled together, copying equations onto little slips of white paper, which they "secretly" refer to during the test.

Social Studies, April 2, 1996

During a test on the history of the midwest, Robbie, Chris, Randy, and Jack enact what they call "the Z system" in taking their multiple-choice test. This works by getting a smart kid to agree to give them the answers to all of the questions. All of the participating students watch the designated student as soon as the tests are handed out. If the student moves his left hand/arm, the answer is "a"; if he moves high right arm/hand, the answer is "b"; if he moves his left leg/foot, the answer is "c"; and if he moves his right leg/arm, the answer is "d." Those students who subscribe to this system must be careful to follow all of the movement in the exact question order, otherwise they will throw off their answers.

Most of the white Canal Town boys regularly participate in actions that are designed to get good grades without having to engage with knowledge. Some of these plans are quite elaborate. Despite the intricacies of "the Z system," for example, the young males achieve rather low grades. Although I focused my observations on the white Canal Town boys and girls, other students were plainly involved in similar practices. As the white Canal Town boys and their classmates sit through class, in many ways, they are disengaged from learning:

Sixth Grade English, January 25, 1996

Teacher reads a short newspaper article to class on how some sixth grade students in Oklahoma were raising money for the families of Oklahoma City bombing victims. She then calls on students, asking them specific questions about the article. Student responses include long pauses, followed by, "Can you read it again?" or "I think I missed that part."

Seventh Grade Science, March 24, 1996

Teacher reviewing a lesson from the previous day on electric circuits, by lecturing and occasionally calling on students to answer questions. Most students do not provide any answer, and when this happens, the teacher offers an explanation, and then asks, "now do you understand?" Students always nod heads and say things like "Oh, I get it now." Students never ask the teacher to elaborate.

For the most part, the young males follow directions while in school, but instead of interacting with knowledge, they pass along the surface of academic work. These students do not disrupt the pace of classroom activity, and, as seen, they hand in homework on time and take tests. As Weis (1990) explains, the Freeway males participate in the form but not the substance of school, which reveals an emerging sense of value in education among white working class males. Although the white high school males in her study express a desire to go to college, large numbers of students did not apply to any form of postsecondary education at all. The Canal Town boys also script secondary education into their futures, but their present academic performance does not quite mirror such goals.

MARRIAGE AND FAMILY

Another facet of identity among the poor white Canal Town boys that has been discussed in previous studies is the emergence of sexism (Willis, 1977; Weis, 1990). Both Willis and Weis demonstrate how white working class young males, in different economies, form a sense of self, in part, around the ideologically constructed identity of females. Willis contends that for the white lads, there are separate spheres in life coded either male or female, and the male sphere is considered superior. Mental labor, for instance, is seen as "feminine" among the lads, and thus less valued. These young men think females should reside in inferior, domestic spaces—cooking and cleaning. The majority of the Freeway males (Weis, 1990) also exhibit sexism in the production of identity, and speak of future wives and children in even more dominant ways.

Because the white Canal Town boys are younger than the "lads" and the Freeway males, their ideas about future wives and families are somewhat vague. When asked, most say they want to be married and have children, but are far away from making any solid plans:

> ROBBIE: I'd like a big house, a wife, and a bunch of kids, I guess . . . I'll be making a lot of money, hopefully, so my wife won't work. She'll take care of the kids, cook, clean. She'll pick up the pizza when I order it too. She won't complain too. . . . I wouldn't want her to work . . . she should be home raising the kids. . . . It's all part of the contract of being married . . . the wife takes care of the husband and the husband gets some free time.

> RANDY: I don't really think about it, but I want to be married, someday. It would be great to come home to a good dinner every night . . . teach your boy about sports. . . . My wife could run to the store for beer, cigarettes, burgers, and pizza when I run out.

> JOHN: Yeah, I'd most likely be married, you know, a house, two cars, a wife, some kids. . . . My wife would do the indoor stuff—you know, cook, clean—and I would do the fun stuff . . . ride snowmobiles, dirt bikes, go out with my friends, get a car, go to Lasertron [laser video arcade], go to the Nine Inch Nails concert [alternative band].

> ANDREW: I don't know . . . I want things normal. I'll be married, with a wife and a few children. . . . I want my wife to be at home and really take care of things. . . . Like, if I had my friends over to watch football or play Nintendo [video game], whatever, she could make snacks and make sure there was cold beer around.

The Canal Town boys articulate the same affirmation of white male supremacy as evidenced in other studies (Willis, 1977; Weis, 1990), in which white females are viewed as objects of male control. For these young males, it is permissible for their wives to work only if there is a financial necessity. Otherwise, it is "normal" for women to be at home, raising children and catering to their husbands' needs, whether it be picking up pizza or supplying snacks and beer while men watch football games on the television. Robbie reifies the notion of separate spheres as he states, "She [wife] should be home raising the kids. . . . It's all part of the contract . . . the wife takes care of the husband and the husband gets some free time." The desire on behalf of these white boys for their wives to reside in domestic spaces is interesting, considering the Canal Town girls want no part in such plans. Instead, the white females view entrance into the public world of paid work as a way to bypass the abuse they feel is scripted into that way of life.

This fantasy future among the Canal Town boys currently exists nowhere in their lives, and is likely fueled by other sources, such as family working class history and media. As media, however, at times presents a more varied image of family and gender roles, it can be argued that vestiges of white working class life—such as the gender roles inscribed in the ideology of the family wage—may remain intact. Smith (1987), for example, argues that the working class family is characterized by the subordination of women to men, as the notion of the family wage was predicated upon the reality that females should receive lower wages than males and/or stay at home. Although industrial jobs are long gone, the poor white Canal Town boys may still be inheriting working class notions of gender arrangements from their families.

DOMESTIC VIOLENCE

Unlike the girls, when asked to describe their community, none of the Canal Town boys mention domestic violence as a defining feature. However, when describing their lives at home and their relationships with girls, these white boys begin to reveal that the females in their lives—mothers, girlfriends, and others in neighborhood—are current victims of abuse. None of these boys are critical about this violence, and most see it as normative. A few, in fact, evidence abusive tendencies themselves. While the Canal Town girls catalogue how they, their mothers, and siblings have been the target of violent outbursts in the past and present, the Canal Town boys do not identify themselves as being victimized. This does not mean, however, that these boys are not on the receiving end of abuse at home.

Through visible bruises and the accounts of neighbors, I do know that a few of the younger white Canal Town boys who are not a part of this cohort are likely the victims of domestic assaults. It is increasingly argued that the nature of relationships between people in families must be understood as highly complex if patterns of domestic violence are to be unraveled (Friedrich & Boriskin, 1976; Gelles & Lancaster, 1987; Justice & Justice, 1990). In fact, it may be that the boys in this investigation experience more violence than their female peers. A child's gender, contend Jouriles and Norwood (1995), potentially greatly affects adult aggressive tendencies toward children. More specifically, it has been found in clinical studies that in cases in which extreme domestic violence is directed toward women, more abuse is inflicted upon sons as compared to daughters. Jourles and Norwood assert that this is likely the case because a child's externalizing behavior often increases the potential of parental aggression toward sons and daughters, and because boys tend to act out more than girls, they are more likely to anger a violent parent and thus end up a primary target of abuse.

As mentioned, although the Canal Town boys do not reveal in this analysis that they are abused themselves, as they describe family relations, they consistently discuss violence in the home in the form of men hitting women. For these white boys, in the dialectical construction of self, they clearly construct white females at home as "other." In many of these instances, the young males see females—their mothers included—as objects of scorn and/or side with adult violent men. What is striking is that none of the boys necessarily flag such situations as wrong and abusive.

> ROBBIE: There's no priority problems in our house except my dad is crabby. They [father and mother] will yell for a couple of minutes and then quit. . . . He pushes her around a little bit, like if the house gets messy or the food is burned. . . . My dad apologizes to her though. He is usually true when he says he's sorry. It's just that she doesn't always do what she's supposed to.

> SAM: I wish they [mother and boyfriend] would stop getting mad . . . like when he comes home late . . . he won't tell my mom where he goes or when he's done and he comes home four hours late. She won't speak to him sometimes. Sometime's I think she's wrong. She should just stop nagging, leave him alone . . . this makes him haul off and swat her. . . . They [females] should give us space. . . . They should also keep away from men's sports. They've already done enough damage. Like Erin.

> CHRIS: I live with my dad; I don't live with my mom. There's four boys and one girl . . . I'm the youngest. . . . My dad works at the gas station [pumps gas in neighborhood gas station]. . . . My sister just moved in with my mom, on another street. . . . My dad and my mom broke up because my mom was doing too much drugs. She was doing drugs when my brother Kurt was in her stomach and it really messed up his brain. The kid that comes in here [the Center] with the dark hair and has a speech problem is my brother. He has tubes in his ears and is slow. She used to do crack and stuff when he was in her stomach. She used to get drunk every night. She does it [crack] now with my sister. She lets my sister do it [crack] with her. She walked out on us when I was 6 months old and my dad takes care of us. . . . Since we're talking about it, I'll say I have my doubts about females . . . they're really mostly good for nothing.

As the Canal Town boys watch relationships between the adult figures at home, they conclude their mothers do not always act as they should. Robbie's exclamation that his mother "doesn't always do what she's supposed to" is a criticism of her housekeeping, which in his opinion, is not as it should be and warrants her being "pushed around." Sam actually sympathizes with his mother's boyfriend—even when he is violent—because his mother, he feels, is a constant nag. Chris, who obviously feels a lot of anger toward his mother, extends his feelings for her to all women. In remarking that females have "already done enough damage" in relation to men's sports, Sam mentions Erin, whom he positions as the target of much resentment, as she was allowed to play a few games on the boys' softball team at the Center a few years ago. When asked about problems with current relationships with white females their own age, in some cases, their potential as present and future female violators becomes apparent.

RANDY: Sometimes . . . they [girls] just don't leave me alone and I want to hit them . . . they keep saying stuff so you just want to turn around and hit them hard. I never did it but I saw my cousin do it. . . . He didn't hit hard though. He got so mad that he just turned around with a left cross and hit her [Tammy]. He hit her in the jaw. Her jaw was numb and she got a fat lip. . . . I get them [females] back on the court or field at school [in gym class]. We run down the field in soccer, and I move and turn the other way, and I give them a little shoot to the back of the knee. Then they'll stop and leave you alone, because they're too busy on the ground crying. . . . After my cousin hit Tammy, nobody else wanted to mess with him. Especially on the court.

ANDREW: I would never hit a girl in my life. I mean I guess only a few times. I dumped her because she was cheating on me. She said she wasn't cheating on me. Then a bunch of people told me she was. It happened about two months ago. But now I'm going back out with her because she called me and told me she's sorry. I really didn't hit her that hard. I smacked her, and I said I would never talk to her again, and don't call my house. And then she called my house and said she was sorry. And now I'm going back out with her.

PETER: They've [females] done enough damage. The NBA women's basketball, the woman goalie first ever in the NHL history, and she throws a shut out . . . they [females] make men look dumb when they do all that. They come into a men's sport out of nowhere and show up. That's bad for your pride. It hurts your pride. . . . It makes guys feel like they want to shoot them or hit them . . . push them up against the lockers at school, smash the locker door in their head . . . give them their softball and leave us alone. . . . How do you think Michael Jordan would feel if one of them college basketball women comes over and dunks him? I don't think he'd feel too good. Six-time MVP; he would feel very bad. Three-time champ. Angry because a woman comes into his sport and dunks over him. People would say that she's better than him and you don't want that to happen because then he would lose his respect. Players would go up to him and laugh because a woman beat him and he's not good anymore because a girl beat him. Then everybody would rub it into his face, call him a girl.

For the Canal Town boys, abuse directed toward females exists in school and in peer relationships, and often revolves around anger over girls playing sports. Randy and Andrew begin by saying they do not hit females, but later in their narrations they demonstrate they do, indeed, inflict violence upon girls. Randy reveals other boys his own age hit girls, for example, his cousin hit Tammy, but "he didn't hit her hard." As Randy indicates, after his cousin hit Tammy, no one "wanted to mess with him. Especially on the court." Andrew feels he was justified in hitting his girlfriend because he heard that she was cheating on him. Peter contends that females are taking over a male domain—athletics. If you lose to a female, you are considered a girl.

Although they do not characterize themselves as targets of domestic violence at home, the boys do reveal their mothers are being abused by adult men. I never once heard any of these young men side with their mothers while describing violent episodes. These boys, instead, think abuse is a normal way to deal with the problems "caused" by females. Just as poor and working class white men are angry that white women will not stay at home, are forcing their way into the workplace, and are stealing "their" jobs (Fine et al., 1997), these much younger white boys are angry at the females in their lives over somewhat similar issues. They have contempt for their mothers, who they say do not take proper care of the home and family, and their female peers, who they think are seeping into what they thought was the sanctioned "male" space of the athletic court. Because of their youth and the normalization of poverty in their lives, a discourse of anger likely does not coalesce around the work world and the loss of jobs. However, by directing anger toward white females for entering sports, these boys may be positioning women as demeaning their imagined future labor.

RACE

Race also emerges as a formidable sphere around which the Canal Town boys construct notions of identity, a finding that is congruent with those of previous studies (Willis, 1977; Weis, 1990; Fine et al., 1997). As revealed by existing research, these young males construct a sense of self in highly individualized ways that are completely removed from deteriorating economic and social relations. As they describe their community and changes over the past few years, they highlight problems—particularly as they are thought to be brought in by those of Puerto Rican and African descent. Like the complaints of the Freeway boys, much expressed racism plays itself out in relation to filth, drug abuse, and crime. Males of African descent are similarly further disparaged for what the Canal Town boys narrate as their repeated attempts to get close to white girls.

> ANDREW: It's [neighborhood] fine, but the garbage that's all around messes the place up. And dirty people, Puerto Ricans, that live around here and in Pepper, start throwing all kinds of stuff into the street. People, like little kids and big people, will smoke and that's the packages of cigarettes you see laying all around and the cigarette butts on the corners. But outside of all that, it's a nice neighborhood.

> JACK: It really wasn't like that a couple of years ago, until all the Puerto Ricans started to move in here. It was a nice neighborhood. It's still a nice neighborhood, except it's getting dirtier and dirtier. And all the people are coming up from the projects and tearing up the Center. . . . Blacks and Puerto Ricans. People from the east side [Puerto Ricans] are moving in here. Some Puerto Ricans take care of their things and do all the things they're supposed to do. They mow their lawn and pick up the stuff that's on the ground near their house. But most of the Puerto Rican houses around here are usually messy. The grass gets huge. It's like they don't care about all the stuff that we worked so hard for. . . . You know, my ancestors digging the canal. It's like the minorities are getting everyone into drugs.

> ROBBIE: Puerto Ricans and Blacks bring in drugs. . . . I don't like how you walk down the street and see kids smoking weed. That just ain't right. They're like 7 and older. . . . The neighborhood's changed. Like Pepper people coming more into Canal Town . . . like the Puerto Rican church that decided to come [no longer in neighborhood]. It was almost an all-white neighborhood, and then it just changed. . . . I don't think other people [white] really like it. A few days ago we [friends] were having a conversation about that. Somebody asked why they [Puerto Ricans] just couldn't stay on the east side . . . and the Blacks trying to get with the girls [white] from here piss us off.

> JAMES: There's lots of racial things here. . . . My brothers totally hate people that aren't their same color. They go up and beat people up for no reason at all. Go up to them and jump them. A couple of weeks ago a Black kid was driving down the street on his bike. My brother Nick punched him in the face as he went by and the kid flew off his bike. Nick's 13. My brother Louie beat one up with a pole for no reason at all. It was pretty bad. The kid was crying. He was walking by and Louie called him a word I can't say. The kid said something back and Louie picked up a pole, ran up to him, and started hitting him with it. I have a little bit of a racist problem because of something that happened in the past with my sister. Kids at school used to try to do a bunch of stuff with my sister. They were all Black and Puerto Rican, so I had a real problem with them. But there's a couple of them that I get along with. Most of them try to act their best.

CHRIS: Whenever I see them [people of African and Puerto Rican descent], they're always talking about white people. But if they act right and got good behavior than I don't got nothing against them. . . . My dad feels the same way. A few months ago, a couple Black kids were walking and I looked back and they started throwing rocks that broke our window [apartment]. We [Chris and father] went out there and they started acting like they were going to jump him [father]. One time in the school yard with my sister, my dad went there to get us and these older Black kids tried to jump him.

SAM: They [Puerto Ricans] live here. . . . The only reason I have problems with them is I've been living in this neighborhood and it's been getting bad with them. They always start trouble with whites for no reason. There's a bunch of Blacks now that moved in from Pepper . . . they started acting racist so I started acting like that; its just the way they've been treating me. I was out on my porch and a bunch of Black kids walked by. They asked what I was doing sitting out here and I told them I live here. Then they started saying a bunch of stuff and swearing at me. But I was ignoring them. Then they picked up rocks and started throwing them at me and chased me. . . . I ran into my yard and they saw the dogs [family pets] back there.

These narrations reveal that for the Canal Town boys, struggles in the formation of identity manifest in virulent racial border patrolling. Andrew, Jack, and Robbie recall how they believe things have changed for the worse because people of African and Puerto Rican descent have started to move in from the Pepper Projects and the east side. According to these boys, homes and properties are deteriorating, the streets are littered with trash, and drug use is on the upswing. Jack is resentful because he feels he can no longer preserve a way of life that was forged by his ancestors. This is the case, he reasons, because those of African and Puerto Rican descent are eroding all that is good about the neighborhood, all of which has historically been maintained by white residents. Andrew and Robbie lament that as a result of these changes, very young Canal Town kids are now smoking cigarettes and marijuana.[5] Again, the narrations of local elders evidence that many of these problems were a part of the history of Irish Americans in the neighborhood.

Many of these young males—such as James, Chris, and Sam—claim they are not racist by nature. All of these boys tell remarkably similar accounts about how while out minding their own business, they have been provoked into fights by African American and Puerto Rican boys. For instance, Sam says he was just sitting on his porch when a group of African American young males started a verbal and physical tirade. In another situation, as Chris contends, for seemingly no reason, African American boys threw rocks at the window of his apartment. James describes how he and his brothers are racist. One of James's brothers brutally attacked a boy of African descent who was riding his bike through Canal Town for "no reason at all." James, however, feels his racism is justified because, as he describes, some African American and Puerto Rican boys were harassing his white sister. In James's view, his entire family has been victimized by African Americans.

In an attempt to understand who they are in their community, these boys describe who they are not. The critique voiced by the Canal Town boys draws the boundaries of acceptable behavior at themselves, and unacceptable behavior at "others." Like the Freeway males (Weis, 1990), many of the white Canal Town boys hold the view that particularly males of African descent are sexually menacing to white community females, and it is, therefore, their duty to protect. One target site for white male anger among these white boys, then, is the sexual realm. However, living in a community in which families are fully displaced economically, the young men also place much importance in funded programs that are offered at, in particular, the Center, and it is around these programs that they lodge the most sustained critique.

> RANDY: It's like, I only hang out with white guys at the Center, but like, in some ways they [Center staff] have to let some Puerto Ricans in . . . I mean, I heard that we need Puerto Ricans here in order to get, like, money, from like, people. Like City Hall won't give money to the Center if it were only white. . . . It [City Hall] gives money to minorities . . . so like we need the Puerto Ricans, which sucks, because it's really about white guys getting screwed over. . . . So, only a couple of Puerto Rican girls come. I really don't have much to do with them being in the gym most of the time. Some of the older guys are really mad about it. . . . I heard them talking . . . they said the minorities can be lazy having a ton of kids and get a ton of money, and if you're white, you're screwed.

> ANDREW: Personally, I can't stand the Blacks and Puerto Ricans. The Blacks don't come here [to Center] so that's one good thing. . . . I don't talk to the Puerto Ricans here. It's really only a few girls that come. . . . Sometimes it's, like, being a minority makes you worth more or something. . . . Like, take Pepper [projects]. The city just spent, like, a load of money fixing it up. If there was whites living there, they would let them fall apart. I hear my dad talking about it . . . people don't care about whites anymore. . . .

> PETER: We [white friends] don't like the Puerto Ricans in the neighborhood because they're involved in drugs and crime, they don't take care of their homes. . . . You hear a lot of older people around here complain about it . . . that the Puerto Ricans get all the breaks; they, like, get more money from the government than whites. All of the sud-

den that more Puerto Ricans have moved into the neighborhood, the Center suddenly gets more money. . . . I don't think it's an accident. . . . I'm glad that it's mostly white here [at Center].

SAM: It's like the ones who take care of the neighborhood don't count, and the ones who are changing things, causing trouble, are rewarded. . . . Like Blacks, Puerto Ricans . . . they're given money to live off of and their kids get more stuff . . . like they have soccer and basketball camp in the summer for free through school. . . . Whites don't get that. . . . You get money if you write down what you want and send it in to, like, officials. They [officials] pick the plan that they think is, like, really important. I guess if you're plain white, your plan don't get picked. It's pretty much like you're worthless.

Expressed racism among the Canal Town boys takes on a quite different shape than that of the white girls. Among these males, there is a well-defined sense of anger that circulates out of a lost sense of felt privilege, all of which lands on entitlement to grant money, funded programs, and so forth. According to Randy, "minorities" are lazy and are getting a "ton" of money in government assistance by having a "ton" of children. In Randy's opinion, the welfare system is catering to such unworthy individuals, and whites—who are not abusing the system—are being passed over. Andrew thinks those of African descent are being favored by those in charge of public funding. He reasons the Pepper Projects have recently been renovated because it is predominantly populated by African Americans.

The discourse narrated by the poor white Canal Town boys reflects personal identities that are completely independent of corroding economic and social relations. This glaring omission was also evident in an earlier chapter, in which elderly Canal Town residents did not blame capital for their economic devastation. This is in particular bold relief, given Canal Town's solid tradition in industry, and the fact that, again, gutted-out warehouses and rusting hulks of steel that used to be factories litter the landscape. Given such immediate and physical testaments to this community's past, it is especially surprising that the elders and the boys do not connect the dilapidated conditions around them to global economic change.

While the Freeway males (Weis, 1990) watched their fathers get laid off from industrial work, because of their youth, by the time the Canal Town boys' fathers came of age, the plants were already closed. As argued earlier, it may be that all hopes of getting a job have been eclipsed long ago. In this context, anger toward "others" swirls around felt lost entitlement to public funds, grants, and assistance. Also previously mentioned, these poor white boys belong to families that all receive some form of government aid, such as food stamps and AFDC.

At the Center, each are part of the dinner program and many families partake in the food bank, while at school, all of the white Canal Town boys participate in subsidized lunches. The young males, additionally, belong to grant-funded year-round recreational leagues at the Center, and participate in Boys' Club, and sponsored dances and skating parties. To an extent, these white boys participate in a number of funded services, yet still feel threatened that "minorities"—who they see as abusing the system—are compromising their entitled access. One could surmise, if this were the case, these boys would likely not be able to avail themselves of so many services/programs.

Inside the bilingual school, the white boys of Canal Town continue their discourse of racial border patrolling. Unlike at the Center, where the majority of those in attendance are white, at the bilingual school, slightly over half of the students are Puerto Rican, the second largest group is white, and only a handful of youth are of African descent. When asked how different groups of kids get along at school, the boys express a considerable amount of animosity toward Puerto Rican and African American students. They believe individuals from such groups to be dangerous, lazy, and favored over whites by those in charge.

ANDREW: We [white students] don't get along with Blacks or Puerto Ricans at all at school. All of them, the ones from the east side, in Canal Town, at Pepper, try to start with us. They're a bad influence on the little kids [white] in the neighborhood and are always bothering some of the girls [white]. . . . Most of them are just sleeping in class and don't do any work.

RANDY: The school had a new addition put on a few years back . . . the part where the cafeteria and auditorium are now, that's the new part. . . . A lot of the grown-ups around here [Canal Town] say that City Hall would never have put a cent into the school if it weren't bilingual, if it were only for whites.

JACK: My mom's boyfriend and his friends both went to [attended] my school a few years back, before it was Spanish. They told me that back then, once in shop class a friend of theirs [white] cut his arm open on the jigsaw blade because there were no blade guards. . . . Back then people in Canal Town passed a sign-up sheet asking to put money into shop class to make it safer. City Hall did nothing. Then they made it [school] into a bilingual school. The first thing they did was they redid the shop class to make it safer. . . . They didn't care if white kids were getting hurt, but they cared that Puerto Ricans weren't.

SAM: The school is getting more dangerous every year. I hear older people tell about how it was to go there like twenty years ago. It was fun, everybody got along, and the school was like a part of the neighborhood. Everyone knew the teachers. . . . Now the teachers are all Puerto

Rican and live on the east side. They could care less about Canal Town. The school is not like a part of Canal Town now. It's like they took the school away from Canal Town, even though it's still in Canal Town. Even the principal is Black. . . . Most of the kids who go there are not from Canal Town. . . . Those kids should have their own school and leave ours alone. We [white people] don't go taking over their school or neighborhood.

The Canal Town boys direct anger toward those of African and Puerto Rican descent for invading their once white neighborhood school; as Sam implores, "Even the principal is Black." As their narrations indicate, the young men learn this anger from older members in the community. These individualized stories of threatened personal and community identity, again, are completely detached from the larger effects of a restructuring economy. While the boys retain an historical sense of anger, they displace it onto "lazy minorities," who are thought to be taking over their once safe, tight-knit community of upstanding citizens, and "City Hall," which is encouraging this to happen. Andrew continues to blame those of African and Puerto Rican descent for harassing white girls and for morally corrupting the white children of Canal Town, as he decrees with indignation, "They're a bad influence on the little kids in the neighborhood." African American and Puerto Rican students, furthermore, claims Andrew, do not put effort into school, preferring instead to sleep or do nothing. Again, even though Andrew and other boys do not seemingly apply themselves to their studies, Andrew draws the line of acceptable behavior in school at his white self.

Although the white Canal Town boys—and some elderly residents—blame both historically available "others" *and* those who hold local positions of power, they cannot see beyond relatively low-level governance. Even though City Hall likely puts its stamp on changes all over Canal Town, the nature of such changes is shaped by more powerful policymakers and a changing economy. The young men, and as they narrate, the adults in their community, never come close to critiquing the brokers of power. In highly individualized ways, the white boys of this community also have harsh words for school policy, which mandates they must learn Spanish.

PETER: My mom and grandfather are mad that they made the school bilingual and that we [white students] are forced to learn Spanish. . . . Whites, like, don't have any choice.

SAM: They should make it so the white kids only have to take Spanish if they want, but that would mean thinking about our [white people's] problems for a change and that ain't going to happen . . . like it's City Hall and people in charge of education who do this shit.

RANDY: Not only did they take our school away, minorities are forcing us [white people] to become less like ourselves, more Spanish. . . . Like my granddad says, when his ancestors came to this country, they had to learn English, so why don't they? [Puerto Ricans] Today, it's all about pleasing the minority.

JOHN: Whatever minorities want they get. Whatever whites want, they lose to minorities. Now they're trying to make their language take over English and City Hall is clearing the way.

Among these poor white boys, there is an extreme desire to point to "others" as the source for the loss of social privilege. Similar to the white Canal Town girls, older family members are seemingly passing these highly personalized, displaced narrations of anger down to these white youth. Yet unlike the girls, these white boys express more consistent anger in their need to sharply draw racial borders. The extent to which these boys feel threatened by people from relatively powerless, culturally oppressed groups is profound, as Randy continues, "minorities are forcing us [white people] to become less like ourselves, more Spanish." The Canal Town boys, along with the elderly residents, are dissatisfied with local government, which they view as ignoring their concerns over those of "minorities."

Through the poor white Canal Town boys' narrations, the strategies involved in patrolling borders comes into sharp focus. Living in a community that has been thoroughly dispossessed economically, the white Canal Town boys feel they are under terrific siege. Expressed resentment toward school authority, and sexist and racist attitudes abound. Sexist and racist behavior of significant proportions emerges as these boys produce identities, and as the white Canal Town boys demonstrate, they are potential abusers of white females and males from culturally oppressed groups, and they view such actions as acceptable. The anger these males direct toward those from culturally oppressed groups, moreover, is channeled into an expressed discourse of lost entitlement to public funding.

In the white space of the community center, the poor white Canal Town boys articulate a highly protectionist discourse in that they want to rid their neighborhood, school, and Center of an African American and Puerto Rican presence. These white boys are indignent, feeling they are being "forced" to accommodate the needs of those from culturally oppressed groups, particularly in school. Angered over having to learn Spanish, the young men keep the language of white siege alive intergenerationally. As Randy comments, "Like my granddad says, when my ancestors came to this country they had to learn English, so why don't they [Puerto Ricans]?" This critique is most desperate and fragile, as

Randy overlooks the fact that his ancestors came from Ireland—an English-speaking country. A closer examination of the school reveals that the institution, indeed, provides a potent ground for such attitudes to strengthen, and sets the stage for a discussion of the important role the Center plays in the lives of poor white Canal Town youth.

CHAPTER 5

The Bilingual School

As seen in the two previous chapters, the poor white Canal Town girls and boys disclose racist attitudes when it comes to those of African and Puerto Rican descent, whom they describe as taking over their neighborhood and school. Through narrations of domestic violence, the white girls evidence personal struggles in the formation of identity around points of gender. However, unlike existing ethnographies of female students, in the comfortable white site of the community center, the girls also reflect upon the culturally diverse spaces of the streets and school with anger. Even though the white girls display more muted racism as compared to the white boys, whose struggles with identity are largely lodged around racial border patrolling, both groups focus considerable energy on the contention that "minorities" are being favored and are "taking over" the neighborhood and school. Despite its status as a bilingual institution—a product of multicultural reform—a similar racialized discourse among white teachers permeates the school.

In this chapter, by focusing mainly on the narrations of white teachers, I explore how the bilingual institution both encourages and contradicts tendencies among the emerging identity of Canal Town youth. I argue that the school presents a terrain that is prime for racist attitudes to grow among these white girls and boys. Of the white female and male teachers interviewed, none are from Canal Town, but all come from working class backgrounds. As they position the bilingual teachers as given more of a voice in how things are done, in their view, the very space of the school provides no outlet in which they can regain a foothold on privileged ground. Similarly, the white Canal Town girls and boys may be acutely expressing animosity toward those from culturally oppressed groups inside the school because the institution seemingly offers no place to escape from "minority favoritism." Constricted by the bounded hours of the school day, white youth cannot freely escape, for example, to the community center to recapture a sense of white privilege. With an emphasis on the form of learning, rather than content, in this school, students are not being prepared for the abstract reasoning needed for mastery of college entrance exams. Perhaps more important, they also are not learning the skills needed to recognize they are displacing anger and are acting out of frameworks that do not serve their interests. Feeling beleaguered and devalued, as the attitudes of the white faculty strongly reflect those of the youth, I assert that this rhetoric of lost entitlement is not just endemic to Canal Town, but instead, has broader appeal.

THE SCHOOL

In the mid-1970s, officials from the State Department of Education and City Hall were looking for an elementary school in the city to develop into a bilingual institution. The new site was to provide an expansion of a bilingual program already established in an elementary school in another part of the city. Both parties settled on the K–8 neighborhood school in Canal Town. The site was purportedly appealing for many reasons, which included a structurally sound facility; a current low enrollment among area youth; a growing local Puerto Rican population; and easy access via a thruway entrance. In September 1979, the refashioned school opened its doors as a bilingual institution to the white and handful of Puerto Rican youth in Canal Town, and to large numbers of Puerto Rican students from the West Side of the city (Board of Education mimeo, 1975).

During the late 1960s and 1970s, bilingual programs were gaining support among mainstream U.S. educators.[1] As many contend (St. Clair et al., 1981; Crawford, 1989; McGroarty, 1992), some members of oppressed groups arguably found a forum in the Civil Rights movements of the 1960s, in which they lobbied for, among other things, a part in shaping the curriculum, pedagogical style, and methods of teaching for their children. Immigration reforms of 1965 resulted in demographic changes in school populations, particularly among groups from Asia and Latin America, adding strength to the demands of the movement. Proponents of bilingual education—who grew in number during this time—reasoned that the institutionalization of native languages acknowledged the legitimacy and power of the community whose language was used.

The bilingual school in this study is part of the Chapter I federal aid program, which is currently funded at $4.3 billion per year. What is now Chapter I evolved from Title I of the Elementary and Secondary Education Act (ESEA), the first major legislation of President Johnson's War on Poverty which was passed by Congress in 1965. The intent of this legislation was to procure services, such as school breakfast programs, additional guidance counseling, and intramural activities, and overall to improve education programs for impoverished youth.

Another objective of Title I was to provide funding for bilingual programs that emphasized English as a second language with the eventual transition to English. Federal funds were disseminated on the basis of school poverty level, while within schools, educational services were to be provided on the basis of individual children's needs. With the intent of reducing the federal role in education, in 1981, the Reagan administration reduced funding and replaced Title I with Chapter I of the Education Consolidation and Improvement Act (ECIA) (Board of Education mimeo, 1975). Today, Chapter I services continue to be provided for students at the bilingual institution, with programming developed by the local school district.

Regarding the school in this study, in its old form as a neighborhood institution serving a shrinking population, most of the space of the building was not being utilized. During its conversion into a bilingual school, the interiors were slightly reconfigured to serve the anticipated increased numbers of students who would come to learn both Spanish and English. For example, three first-floor classrooms were adapted into language laboratories, and small enclosed offices were built in several rooms to provide a private place where students could practice their language skills out loud. Storage space taking up the entire second floor was cleared and transformed into classrooms for seventh and eighth graders. As mentioned, during the 1995–96 academic year, the total student population was 466. Of these students, 43 percent were white, 54 percent were Puerto Rican, and 3 percent were African American. Broken down by gender, 52 percent of the students were female, while 48 percent were male. Students of African descent from the bordering Pepper Projects attended another public school.[2]

At the time of the school's conversion, in order to serve the swelling ranks of students, most teachers retained their positions, although a few were reassigned to other institutions. The number of faculty members, however, basically doubled, as Spanish-speaking staff and teachers for every grade level were hired.[3] Today, all of the teachers on the faculty at the bilingual institution who experienced the school's transformation firsthand have retired. A few of those teachers, I am told, had been residents of the Canal Town community. Currently, none of the teachers at the bilingual school are from the area. According to city documents, for the 1995–96 school year, 55 percent of the teachers were white and 45 percent of the teachers were Puerto Rican. Of those teachers, 60 percent were female and 40 percent were male (Board of Education mimeo, 1997).

Except for the principal, there were no faculty members of African descent at the bilingual institution during this study. African American women did have positions as front office personnel and cafeteria staff.

Although I do not largely focus on the narrations of Puerto Rican teachers in this chapter, the six who were interviewed said they lived on the east side, and many had children enrolled in the school. Among these teachers, five migrated from Puerto Rico to this city over the past fifteen years, while one was born on the mainland. Regarding the six white teachers, five revealed they lived in a section of the city to the north of Canal Town, while one lived in a suburban area further north. None of the white teachers reported having children in attendance at the school. Through personal interviews, each of the six white teachers said they had historical connections to working class life in this city. All of these individuals narrated they had fathers, grandfathers, older brothers, and uncles who labored in a variety of the former industry within and nearby Canal Town. Only one white male participant reported he had direct experience working in industry himself—while paying for college, he said he worked summer jobs in the steel plants and grain elevators of Canal Town.

Three years ago, the Board of Education hired a new principal at the bilingual school, a middle-age woman of African descent, named Mrs. Martin.[4] The former principal, a Puerto Rican male, decided to vacate his position after he was offered an administrative job in Detroit. In an individual interview, Mrs. Martin told me she taught for ten years in city public schools, and this was her first appointment as a principal. Mrs. Martin also said there was controversy in the school over her hire because many teachers wanted a principal who was bilingual, and she did not know Spanish. The situation was "handled," said Mrs. Martin, by the school board's decision to hire a Spanish-speaking assistant to the principal, named Mrs. Delgato. The year in which I conducted my research was the second year Mrs. Delgato had been on the job. A young woman of Puerto Rican descent who lived on the east side, Mrs. Delgato had an extensive background as an administrative assistant in city schools, and presently had two children of her own enrolled at the bilingual institution. An office was cleared for Mrs. Delgato in a room adjacent to a former resource room.

As stated, one goal of this K–8 bilingual school is to prepare Spanish-speaking students for quick transition into English, while exposing English-speaking students to the linguistic practices and cultures of Spanish-speaking people (Bilingual Education mimeo, 1990). There are, however, two "tracks" at this school, a bilingual track and an English track, with an equal number of students in each track. According to Mrs. Martin, students are assigned to tracks, with the general rule that Spanish-speaking students are placed in the Spanish track as it is geared toward English proficiency. These two tracks are in place from kindergarten through grade six. The Spanish track is dissolved in the seventh and eighth grades, where there is only an English track available. This arrangement has proven problematic for seventh and eighth grade students who have recently arrived from Puerto Rico speaking only Spanish.

In terms of public relations, it can be said that the past year has been difficult for the bilingual institution in Canal Town. I learned from a number of teachers that the previous year, a group of English track faculty went over the principal's head, and complained to the school board that teachers' aides were being unfairly assigned to only bilingual teachers. In addition, in the late fall of my observation year, a Puerto Rican female fifth grade teacher was indicted as part of a heroin ring, and dramatically, was handcuffed and taken away to the city police station in front of her class. This event was widely publicized on the local television news and in the newspaper. For these reasons, and perhaps others, as will be seen, teachers at the bilingual school are of the opinion that the principal does not fully trust the faculty.[5]

In this chapter, I explore how daily life at the bilingual institution impacts upon the construction of identities as displayed among Canal Town girls and boys in earlier chapters. As will be seen, in terms of viewing education, a paradoxical understanding of schooling is advanced. With an emphasis on form and control at the level of principal and teacher interaction, in a dialectical way, this tempers the treatment and presentation of knowledge by teachers in classrooms, and the ways in which youth come to perceive schooling and knowledge. With energies directed toward the maintenance of form, the notion of critically engaging with knowledge is lost, even as teachers forward the message that higher education clears the threshold to a good life. Also lost, therefore, is the potential for youth to begin to critically examine their social positions. In many ways, the institution also provides a breeding ground for the racist attitudes seen among the Canal Town youth. As they participate in the construction of separate gender/race spheres, the white female and male teachers narrate the school as being "taken over" by Puerto Rican faculty. In the view of the white teachers, they are being deeply pushed into the tight corners of the institution.

PARADOXICAL VIEWS OF SCHOOLING

In the many sixth, seventh, and eighth grade classes I observed at the bilingual institution over a span of an academic year, teachers tend to embrace the form rather than the substance of learning, which mirrors findings in earlier research on the distribution of knowledge in working class schools (Anyon, 1983; McNeil, 1986; Weis, 1990). By not learn-ing to engage in critical reflection, youth are not being equipped in school with the tools needed to dismantle their economic dislocations as socially and historically constructed. At least in the upper grades, although higher education is emphasized as important, the teachers describe college as something to be merely traded in for a job, and in pri-vate conversation, many confess they do not think their students are postsecondary school material. This paradoxical thinking about higher education among teachers is seemingly part of the practice of both English track and Spanish track faculty.

Eighth Grade Math, April 20, 1996

At the start of class, Mrs. West hands out a worksheet to be done dur-ing the period. Students groan. Teacher says they are "lucky" because she could give it out for homework. Mrs. West: "You [students] are also lucky because if you weren't in here [school] you would probably be out on the streets doing God knows what. . . . If you want a good life, you need a good job. If you want a good job, you have to go to college. If you want to go to college, you have to be disciplined."

Seventh Grade homeroom, February 23, 1996

MR. GARCIA: [Talking to me before morning bell]. "Many of these kids have no respect, no values. A lot treat their teachers like crap and they disrespect their parents. It's starting earlier and earlier. Taking drugs, drinking, having sex at sixth grade. The parents aren't doing their job. They're [students] not taught values in the home. Absent fathers, mothers who are doing drugs and giving it to their kids, mothers who prostitute themselves. I don't understand it. I grew up in a poor fam-ily, but we learned the difference between right and wrong. My parents cared about me. I can't say the same for these parents. . . . I try to inter-est them in college, so they can get jobs and a stable life, but I know it probably won't happen for them. . . . I basically consider it a success story when I hear that one of my former students graduates from high school and joins the army, or when a girl graduates without getting pregnant."

Eighth Grade Science, April 3, 1996

MR. HOWELL: Do you think you can get into, let alone pass college without following the rules? College is all about rules. You have to show up to class, do your assignments, take exams. The minute you slack off you get thrown out. Your shot at a good job goes down the drain. Trust me guys, you got to learn now. I'm not telling you this for my own good. [After class Mr. Howell tells me that it's "sad" because he knows most of these students will not go on to college.]

Although higher education is positioned as key to a "stable life," teachers do not have high expectations for their students. Mrs. West, for example, is of the opinion that without a rigid structure provided by school, students would likely "be out on the streets doing God knows what." Concerning what he sees as a lack of respect among students, Mr. Garcia mentions his modest upbringing, and devoid of talk of the demise of industry and the types of jobs once available, blames parents for not doing their job. Mr. Howell is forthright about his belief that many students will not make it to college. Mrs. West and Mr. Garcia nearly ascribe biological characteristics to their students in contending they come from bad families and/or are just plain bad.

Not only do these teachers think higher education is unobtainable for their students, it is portrayed as a commodity to be exchanged on the market for a job. None of these teachers emphasize learning in college as important. For Mrs. West, a good life is the equivalent of a good job, and a good job can only be secured by postsecondary education. Mr. Garcia and Mr. Howell also view a stable life as an outcome of college attendance. Among none of these teachers is there an analysis of present corroding economic and social relations and the value of a college diploma in the current economy.

Just as these teachers contend that higher education equals discipline and "college is all about rules," similar sentiments guide the form of knowledge in classes at the bilingual school. Rote learning and memorization are the norm, not critical thinking or engagement with material, which are skills needed for mastery of college entrance exams. McNeil (1986) finds that students are not taught they can take ownership over their own learning and create knowledge. It is arguably these skills which the Canal Town youth will need if they are to break out of their ahistorical search for someone to blame. At the bilingual institution, lessons typically revolve around structured notes or worksheets which do not offer much room for discussion.

Eighth Grade English, January 25, 1996

Mr. Peak is reviewing for a unit test on the book, *The Outsiders*. The review consists of overheads on which are photocopied multiple-choice questions related to plot. During the first twenty-five minutes of class, teacher has students take out a sheet of blank paper and silently select answers on their own. Students are then told to exchange papers and mark each other's work while he reads the answers. Mr. Peak: [At the end of class]. "Okay, if you know this stuff, you know the book. You might not all be geniuses, but you're all capable of memorizing this stuff."

Sixth Grade Spanish Track Science, April 12

[Lesson on the reproductive cycle of a flower. Teacher tapes a poster of a flower to front chalkboard.] Mr. Mateo: "All right, open to page 95 [in the textbook] and get out a loose leaf sheet of paper for notes. Put the title 'Reproduction-Flower' at the top of the page and underline it." Teacher points to parts of flower and calls on students to look in book for the corresponding name of the part and to read aloud its function in the reproduction process. Teacher has students copy down this information, exactly as it is in the book, on their papers.

Sixth Grade English Track Spanish, May 2

Mrs. Diaz has students add twenty new words to their "vocabulary notebooks." The words are listed on the board. Students have to copy down the words ten times each in their notebooks. For homework, students have to write out the definitions of the new vocabulary words, which as directions indicate, are to be found in the back of the book.

In the one-day review of *The Outsiders*, there is no room for students to critically think about the story itself and larger themes, such as human nature and motivation. They are told, rather, that if they can correctly fill in the blanks, then they "know" the book. The lesson on flower reproduction consists of transferring definitions verbatim from the textbook to student notes, in an extremely rigid manner—even the title of the notes are supplied. During the entire unit on plant reproduction, the teacher never has students make sense of the reproduction process themselves. In Spanish class as well, students are told to copy down words, and are given no time to think through their meanings and uses. These class excerpts were far from unusual; the tenor of most lessons throughout fieldwork, in fact, consisted of copying notes, making lists, and filling in blanks. At no point during my stay in the field did I notice a student challenge knowledge as presented. The only student interruptions were to ask for further clarification of an assignment. One day after class, Mrs. Diaz, a relatively new sixth grade teacher, only in the profession three years, articulated a critique of the codified forms that knowledge takes at this school.

I would like to do more with the students. I believe some students could make something of themselves if given the opportunity. . . . It's just that every year we're given more responsibilities; more is added to the curriculum. In the beginning [when I started teaching], I had big ideas. I was going to have skits and role playing. I was going to bring literature and music to the class. And I did do those things for a year, but they fell apart. The students just saw it as an opportunity to goof off. They got disrespectful. Some of the older teachers advised me to have strict lectures, lots of drills. I do find these students want order, a sense of structure in their lives. It's sad; the second you give them an inch, they take a mile. . . . The parents aren't doing their job, and we [teachers] can't teach our students what the parents should be [teaching them]. . . . Anyway, I've also learned that if you want to have people on your side [other teachers], you have to do things the way other people do them. I know at least five tenured teachers in this school who just do dittos on the overhead, day in, day out. You can't just waltz into a school and change things . . . they [school board] hired me because of my forward thinking, but then I was punished for it when I started my job. . . . They [professors] didn't tell us about that in college.

Mrs. Diaz is highly critical of the workaday aspect of teaching and learning at this school and believes on some level she is doing a disservice to her students. As she describes the shift between her teacher preparation courses and the realities of her actual assignment, Mrs. Diaz explains how her teaching style has changed. From laboriously unpacking the already overstuffed curriculum, to handling discipline problems, to struggling to being accepted by her colleagues, this teacher reveals how, on a practical level, she is submitting to the brand of teaching at the institution, which is characterized by student control. In some ways, Mrs. Diaz has come to think this teaching style is best suited for this population of students, who "want order, a sense of structure in their lives."

As previously discussed, although Canal Town youth occasionally cause disturbances, the structure of the school day is not challenged. The goal in schooling for these middle school adolescents, moreover, is simply to "pass." Resembling McNeil's findings (1986), students and teachers alike are taken up with the form of knowledge, but not its substance. Meaningful classroom discussion over knowledge does not occur because of the heavy template of form set in place in class. Although Canal Town girls, boys, and bilingual school teachers agree that college is the foundation of a secure life, it is not the knowledge that may be learned that is coveted. The diploma, instead, is positioned as most important. While a lack of engagement in complex thinking may not prohibit these students from obtaining a high school diploma, they are not being prepared to do well on college entrance exams. Unversed in critical analysis and abstract reasoning, these students most likely will also not be admitted to the type of institutions of higher learning which serve as an entranceway into middle-class life.

The school, then, promotes the contradictory attitude toward school culture and knowledge that surfaces among Canal Town girls and boys by emphasizing the utilitarianism of schooling and the transmission of highly structured knowledge. As part of the tacit contract of "passing," students must sit through a one-dimensional form of learning. In this way, the institution can be seen as having a hand in the shaping of historically working class notions of schooling. In this institution, these youth are seemingly not learning the analytical skills needed to help them begin to view their social realities as historically constructed.

CONTROL OVER TEACHER LABOR

The emphasis on form, at the expense of content and meaningful engagement with material, occurs on many levels at the bilingual institution. Similar to McNeil's research (1986), control in the institution surfaces both as it relates to the distribution of knowledge and teacher labor. As evidenced in observations and interviews with teachers, in this school, there is chronic tension between the faculty and the principal, Mrs. Martin. As a relatively new principal in a school in which there are no vice principals, Mrs. Martin is a convenient figure to blame. As learned from the articulations of the teachers, this animosity primarily emerges in relation to two aspects of the principal's leadership style: her control over plan books, and her habit of walking in on classes unannounced for "spot discipline checks." As the principal exerts control over teacher labor, teachers likewise tightly control the form and distribution of learning in their classrooms.

Weis (1990) concludes that in some notable ways, the relationship between administrators and teachers at Freeway high school resembles that of teachers and students. In Freeway, administrators exercise a degree of control over the form of teacher labor to such an extent that the substance of what is taught is wholly ignored. Yet, through the strict regulation of plan books, audiovisual equipment, photocopying, and door window coverings, there is a feeling of profound control over teacher practice. Weis raises the point that this emphasis on form at the administrative level may contribute to the contradictory attitude toward schooling and school knowledge that was evident among youth. As administrators emphasize form, in a dialectical act of production, teachers may also emphasize form in their classrooms. I suggest that similar practices play out in the bilingual school. A major area of struggle in teacher-administrator interaction in this school also involves the preparation of plan books.

> MR. PERRY: It's like, some of us have been teaching for twenty years and then suddenly [with the hire of Mrs. Martin] we're told how to plan out work. . . . The plan books have to be done a certain way, as

if it was getting graded. . . . We [teachers] work hard . . . we're not treated like we're competent. . . . She [principal] has no trust in our ability.

MRS. DIAZ: I don't mind doing plan books, we spent a lot of time in college learning the importance of organizing and planning material. . . . It's just that our principal has us do some things that are, well, a little insulting . . . like after we're done writing out our plans, we have to underline our lesson objectives with a red pencil. During orientation, she [principal] read the definition of the word "objective" from a dictionary and asked us to write it down. At the beginning of the school year we [teachers] all got red pencils in our mailboxes.

MR. HOURS: I believe that I'm a good teacher. I just try to do my best. By doing my plan book the way she [principal] wants it, you know, I feel like I'm not being trusted. . . . I've been to graduate school; I was a top student.

Rigid control over plan books deemphasizes any meaningful engagement with the content of knowledge as presented in class. Even if done to satisfaction, it is uncertain if the plan books have any connection to the substance and treatment of material. Such actions simply give the appearance of order and control. Mr. Perry, a seventh grade social studies teacher; Mrs. Diaz; and Mr. Hours, a seventh grade math teacher, are all insulted by the principal's plan book instructions. They feel they are being patronized instead of treated like professionals in having to fulfill this task. The teachers at the bilingual school are also angered because they do not receive feedback on their efforts.

MRS. WEST: It makes a lot of us mad because not only do we go through all this trouble to do our plan books a certain way, with colored pencils and everything, we don't get a report telling us, you know, like "these plans look great." You just don't get rewarded, even if it's just like a little praise. You don't know how you're doing, so you can't improve. The only time you know is if you don't do them right, you get a form letter in the mail saying basically "do your plan books right or else."

Although teachers must submit their plan books to the principal biweekly, they say they receive no sense of how they are doing with this task. As the teachers are given no feedback, this may be linked on another level to the school's encouragement of contradictory attitudes toward schooling and school knowledge among Canal Town youth. Since correct completion of the job requires simply handing in plan books finished to specification every two weeks, this may be yet another example of attention to form without emphasis on any meaningful analysis of content. In an interview with the principal, I asked about the plan book policy.

> MRS. MARTIN: It has really turned out well [the evaluation of plan books]. You see, I wanted to streamline. . . . In this school there are the bilingual teachers doing their thing, and the other teachers doing their thing. . . . We've suffered [at this school] from some bad PR [public relations] in the eyes of the board of education. . . . My goal is to make this school's reputation rise above that. To do this, you've got to crack down and show that you mean business.

Turning in plan books is justified by the principal as a method of "streamlining" the faculty at the bilingual school. The principal reveals that she sees the bilingual teachers and the "other" teachers as separate groups, a mere hint at the tensions among faculty that will soon be explored at length. Also mentioned by the principal is the recent bad press from which the school has lately suffered. Mrs. Martin's plan to regain a solid reputation is to "crack down" on those teachers who she thinks are, perhaps, not up to par. By tightly regulating plan books, Mrs. Martin seemingly gets the sense of being in control, while actually paying little attention to the substance of what is presented in class. The teachers, however, see this form of administrative control as trivial.

Another source of antagonism between teachers and the principal at the bilingual school is Mrs. Martin's habit of regularly walking into classes unannounced to do what she calls "spot discipline checks." According to some teachers, while so doing, Mrs. Martin has been known to publicly tell a teacher to "crack down" on discipline on the spot. Other times, some teachers contend, she stands in the back of the room "frowning" at what she determines as unruly behavior. Teachers discussed the uncomfortable nature of these visits with each other often—during lunch and between classes. Not only do the teachers express they feel they are being controlled by an administration that has little trust in their abilities as professionals, they complain they are being undermined in front of their students.

> MR. PEAK: It's, like, Martin just shows up whenever she feels like it, sometimes she sneaks in and you don't even notice it . . . that's why I teach only with my door closed now. . . . It would be, like, you were teaching facing the class, and then you'd turn and she was suddenly learning against the chalkboard for God knows how long. . . . Then she says things like, "Mr. Peak, I think you have someone sleeping in the back row." So she's telling me, someone who's been teaching for fif-

teen years, how to manage my class, in front of my class! . . . Now I only teach with my door shut; this way I can at least hear her when she lets herself in.

MRS. WEST: She [principal] walks in when she wants, and if she sees students talking even for a second, she reprimands not the student, but the teacher, right then and there. Once she said out loud, "Miss West, I'd like to see you after class," as if she were making an appointment with a problem student! She proceeded to tell me after class to get better control over the class. . . . Oh, the kids know it. They know that I'm going to get a talking to. They notice everything. It makes me look like someone with no authority. These "discipline checks" actually make students more undisciplined. They think, "Why should we do what she says? She [teacher] even gets in trouble with Mrs. Martin."

MRS. DIAZ: Ever since Mrs. Martin came, no one's [teachers] comfortable. They have to make sure Mrs. Martin isn't around all the time; many teachers are fearful. She walks in classes in the middle of teaching. It makes me nervous. She walks up and down the rows, still while I'm teaching and points to, say, a piece of garbage on the floor, and stares at a student. They know it's a signal to get up and throw it out right away. She taps others on the shoulder, which means sit up straight. . . . It makes me feel that I'm not doing a good job. One day she even made a whole row of students line their desks up better. I get so uncomfortable when she's in my room; I'm positive the kids sense this. It's like they're afraid of her, but they are also amused that I get so nervous. It's just that she always frowns.

This emphasis on control results in conflict taking place only around issues of form, which serves to level off any meaningful struggle that might take place over, for example, the selection and treatment of knowledge. Both veteran teachers such as Mr. Peak and newer teachers such as Mrs. Diaz feel their trustworthiness as highly educated professionals is being called into question. Not only do they resent this invasion of their classroom space by the principal, but their notion of what constitutes good teaching and learning has come to be measured by their success at establishing order and control. Contextualized in an atmosphere in which form is highly regulated, the goal of students schooled in this climate is to "pass." Again, by short-circuiting meaningful engagement with the substance of knowledge, students are not being prepared to do well on college entrance exams, thus the potential for entry into middle-class life is seriously limited. The Canal Town students, furthermore, are also not learning the skills needed to constructively engage in meaningful critique, and their desperate scramble to maintain their assumed sense of privilege goes on uninterrupted at school. So, despite this school's status as a bilingual institution—which relies upon the illusion of innovation and multiculturalism—the presentation of knowledge, and in particular, the obsession over form and control, differs little from that of other schools serving poor youth.

RACE/GENDER DIVISIONS

Although the teacher culture at the bilingual school resembles that of other institutions, a highly racialized discourse also informs ways in which space is managed. Similar to other work (McNeil, 1986), in the bilingual school, there are separate spheres structured along lines of gender and race, which guide a set of messages about the normality of behaviors and attitudes at this institution. Although the white and Puerto Rican female teachers occasionally come together around gender struggles, upon closer analysis, it is also the case that the white female and male teachers interpret the faculty of Puerto Rican descent as "colonizing" the spaces of the school, and leaving those who are white with no place to go. This theme among white teachers parallels the notion among Canal Town youth that "minorities" are "taking over." Feeling trapped in an institution they believe demands endless compromise by white teachers, a sustained racist discourse surfaces around two central issues: the hiring of Mrs. Delgato and the assigning of teachers' aides.

In the bilingual school, the formation and maintenance of separate gender spheres emerge in the few spaces where teachers have the opportunity to get together, for example, at staff meetings, in the morning before class, in the faculty lounge, and during lunch. In the bilingual institution, at times, both white and Puerto Rican male teachers enter "female" space. Not once during my observations did female teachers "transgress" gender lines. This phenonemon mirrors the working class allotment of space, in which males avail themselves of the public and domestic spheres as they choose, while women are conditioned to stay in only the domestic sphere. These patterns of gender/race segregation were detectable throughout the duration of my stay at the school, and were first noticed at a staff meeting in early September, which was held in the school auditorium:

September 1

Teachers mingling with each other in small groups that are gender and race specific. A group of white male teachers is at the front of the auditorium. A group of white female teachers is standing near a table at the front; a few are filling coffee cups. A group of Puerto Rican female teachers is already seated in a cluster in the first few rows on the right-hand side. A few of the women are passing around pictures of their children, vacations. Two of the Puerto Rican women get up and get coffee for their group. They talk and joke around with some of the white women for about ten minutes while getting the coffee and then go back to their seats. A group of Puerto Rican male teachers is standing to the far right of the Puerto Rican women. White and Puerto Rican male teachers occasionally leave their groups to get some coffee and come right back. After about twenty minutes, Mrs. Martin calls the meeting to order. Everyone sits down in the same gender and race specific clusters. The Puerto Rican men sit to the left of the Puerto Rican women. The white female teachers fill the left side of the first few rows. The white male teachers sit in the first few rows of the left wing. Everyone is speaking in English.

Although individual women and men break out of their "groups" and talk to other teachers, they always return to their original cluster of friends, whom they eventually sit with throughout the meeting. In terms of interaction between cohorts, the Puerto Rican and white women engage in more sustained exchanges with each other as compared to the men, whose conversation is almost nonexistent.

At the bilingual institution, white and Puerto Rican female teachers, who normally exist in separate racial spheres, tend to interact more than the white and Puerto Rican male teachers—and at times they rally around issues of what they think are gender inequalities within the school. As I observed, teachers were needed throughout the year to organize events and activities such as the PTA, the annual student fund-raising drive, and the eighth grade graduation. On numerous occasions, over lunch and in individual interviews, female teachers are angry that the male faculty just "assume" women will be willing and available to volunteer. In one example during lunch, four white female teachers talk about how busy they are, which leads into a discussion about faculty gender inequity and how female faculty have to "help out" more. A female teacher of Puerto Rican descent joins in the conversation, which sparks a dialogue between the two tables around this point.[6]

Lunch, November 28

MRS. WEST: It's not that I mind working extra with the kids in being the faculty fund-raising rep[resentative], but it's just, like, lots of work; that's lots of money to be responsible for. What gets me about it is that none of the guys ever volunteer for the job. Somehow, a female faculty always gets the job.

MRS. FERRY: [Eighth grade social studies teacher] That's because they [men] think women are natural born helpers. . . . I get it at home and here; where's the justice?

MRS. HERNANDEZ: [From two tables behind] I couldn't help hearing that one, Mary [Mrs. West]. I know I've never seen one of the guys [male teachers] work the bake sale table during open house. I always know I'll end up doing it.

MRS. WEST: Yeah, it's always the women that have to do the little things, only they're not so little. . . . Sometimes it's not easy; sometimes when one more thing is piled onto the day, like making sure hundreds of order forms are handed in, you just want to rest, but you can't. You've got to go home and cook dinner, pick up the kids, clean up, grade papers, think about tomorrow.

In another example from an individual interview, Mrs. Stefanski shares her feelings on this subject.

MRS. STEFANSKI: The eighth grade graduation is a ton of work . . . yeah, Mrs. Hernandez and I have done it for, let's see, for at least the last six years. . . . There has to be an English and bilingual coordinator, so there's two of us. . . . It's that now no one ever asks us to do it, they just assume, I guess that we'll do it. . . . Now that I think about it, most of the female teachers are attached to some large extra project, like leading the fund drive or something or other. . . . I guess I should be really mad because the guys don't do anything to the point that they're not even asked anymore. It's a waste of breath . . . I guess our principal knows the women will always say "yes."

These white and Puerto Rican female teachers are critical of male faculty inside the school and in relation to what they think is the unfair distribution of "extra" work as related to the job.

Interestingly, although they think it is wrong that the men do not take on any "extra" school duties, these women ultimately blame the principal for enlisting them to volunteer. The critique of patriarchal relations, it seems, is deflected off the men and onto another woman—Mrs. Martin. Still, the female teachers, particularly the white women, continually assist males in school with domestic tasks, such as getting coffee and operating a microwave oven during lunch. The instances of women coming together across cultures are not all that common, and among the white teachers interviewed, a racist discourse also emerges, which seemingly weakens any collective gender critique.

At the bilingual institution, teachers usually arrive each day to school about a half hour before students. After checking mailboxes, getting coffee, and making photocopies, white male and Puerto Rican male teachers characteristically stay in their respective classrooms, preparing lessons and grading papers. Comparatively, after taking care of morning tasks, white female teachers almost always gather in small clusters outside their classroom doors to talk. White women seemingly gather with those white women whose classrooms are closest, therefore, primary grade teachers talk with other primary grade teachers, and so forth. As Mrs. West explains, these few minutes of socializing are a routinized part of the job.

> MRS. WEST: I talk a little with Mrs. Stefaniski [seventh grade English teacher] every morning out in the hall. I don't know; I guess we talk about what we made for dinner, what was on TV, how the driving was [depending upon weather conditions] coming in from her side of town. ..'s a regular part of the day. . . . It would be strange if we didn't talk a little like we do . . . it would be like something wasn't right . . . I mean, we're not like the Puerto Rican women, who, like, almost establish their own little colony every morning.

According to Mrs. West, the female Puerto Rican teachers step over the line of acceptable behavior each morning as they "almost establish their own little colony." The Puerto Rican female faculty do engage in a much more elaborate ritual to ease them into the day. All of these women gather as one large group in the room outside the office of Mrs. Delgato every morning. The space, which used to be a former resource room, is furnished with a couch and a number of tables and chairs. In an individual interview, I asked Mrs. Hernandez, a sixth grade Spanish track teacher, to tell me about this habit. As she describes it, there is seemingly a sense of familiarity among many of the Puerto Rican female teachers, the extent of which I did not observe among the white female teachers. Some of this may stem from the fact that most of the Puerto Rican female faculty live on the same streets in the same upper west side neighborhood. As explained by Mrs. Hernandez, many of the women are involved in each other's lives both inside and outside school.

> I guess it's [meeting in the morning] just, like, to touch base, you know? To, like, check in with each other. A lot of us [Puerto Rican women] ride in with each other. A number of us have enrolled our kids in this school and they ride in with us. . . . We have our own coffee pot; we take turns bringing in coffee cake or something we baked. . . . It's kind of like our own little place to, like, go to. . . . We can, like, prepare for the day . . . I mean, we get together. It's not just here but at home; our kids play together.

I spent many mornings with the Puerto Rican female teachers in this space, and noticed that Puerto Rican male teachers would temporarily break into this room, for example, to get a slice of coffee cake, and then leave. I never saw white men or white women attempt to come into this sphere, which suggests that spaces coded Puerto Rican and female are the domain of Puerto Rican males. Teacher aides, office personnel, and cafeteria staff who are female and of Puerto Rican descent also occasionally visit with the Puerto Rican women in this space during the day.[7]

Regarding the use of the faculty lounge, white female and white male teachers regularly visit.[8] Inside this space, white women tend to sit on the chairs and couch in the back right-hand corner of the room. While white males occasionally sit with the white women in the back of the room, I never saw a woman sit up front with the men. Although Puerto Rican males do enter the lounge, they do not typically do so, and in general, spend their breaks alone in their classrooms. During the instances when a Puerto Rican male teacher did go to the faculty lounge, he seemed to only come with a purpose, for example, to talk to a teacher about audiovisual equipment. The Puerto Rican men stayed exclusively in the "male" space when they did come, and hardly ever entered the part of the room where the white women sat. When the white teachers were asked why they chose to spend their free minutes in the lounge, their answers suggest that they have no choice, having been squeezed out of other places by "minorities."

> MR. PERRY: It's like we [white teachers] know that we belong here [in lounge]. Because this is a bilingual school. Let's just say that minorities have more of a voice. Some people think they should have this [more of a voice]; I don't know. We [white teachers] really don't ask for things like our own lounge, because, face it, they [administrators] focus on the bilingual aspects of the school. . . . I've been in this system long enough to know that we [white teachers] wouldn't get a special lounge like the Puerto Rican women have. We have to make do. I'm used to it . . . it's the way the system was set up.

> MRS. STEFANSKI: We [white friends] really don't have any alternatives if we want to go somewhere to talk with other faculty. . . . A lot of that is because this is a bilingual school, so it's like the plans for the way things get done get set by the bilingual teachers . . . it's just the way it is. . . . I can barely walk around without knocking into someone back here [of lounge].

> MR. HOURS: Part of teaching in a bilingual school is that you have to realize that the bilingual teachers will have more of a say in how things are done. I mean, you've got to expect it from the administration. I mean, with our free periods, we're [white teachers] here [in the lounge]; we've really got no place to go.

> MRS. WEST: This is a really small lounge for a whole lot of people. I taught at a regular public school in _____ [city] for twelve years before coming here. When I first came here, I wasn't used to how

things were done at a bilingual school. To be honest with you, in the beginning, I felt I was being forced into this lounge . . . I felt like this was the only place where the English-speaking teachers should be. Sometimes I still feel this way. I mean, it's pretty cramped back here.

These white teachers contend that the walls of the bilingual institution are closing in on them. They believe the administrators and Puerto Rican teachers have taken over the school, and are responsible for their "marginalization" inside the faculty lounge. While the white female teachers are convinced that the school agenda is controlled by bilingual teachers, the white male teachers point to an administration that favors "minorities." This discrepency between females and males over who controls school space may be linked to the historical tendency among white working class males to challenge authority—a distinction that was seen among the Canal Town girls and boys as they make sense of school forms and meanings. Although these faculty describe the lounge as a "cramped" space controlled by "minorities"/administrators, none of the white women see themselves and the white men as partaking in the production of separate spheres within the room. Nowhere in these narrations, additionally, is there a critique that the lounge is one of the few legitimized spaces inside schools for teachers, and it is the Puerto Rican females and males who found alternative spaces for themselves.

These gender/race patterns and attitudes also emerge in the lunchroom. During mealtime, the white female teachers always sit at a table in the middle of the faculty cafeteria, while the Puerto Rican female teachers consistently sit two tables behind them, at the back of the room. White male teachers sit at the table on the left that is closest to the lunch line, and the Puerto Rican male teachers sit at the table on the right that is nearest to where lunch is purchased. This seating pattern was sustained throughout the duration of my observations of the teachers in the higher grades at this school. I had occasion to visit the faculty lunchroom during earlier periods when catching up on field notes, and during that time, I noticed that teachers in the primary grades took part in this same gender/race grouping. When asked about these seating arrangements, the white teachers in this study, again, were of the opinion that the teachers of Puerto Rican descent were self-segregating and "taking over."

MR. PEAK: The bilingual teachers, the guys, like to sit by themselves and speak Spanish. They really don't have much in common with us. They don't watch _____ [football team] games or hockey. It's a cultural thing that they only like soccer. . . . They should, you know, not speak Spanish at lunch. It excludes us.

MRS. STEFANSKI: The Puerto Rican teachers, some of them are real nice. Like a couple of the women. They like to be loud, though, and keep with their own. . . . That's the thing that really bothers me. They're so loud that they, like, take over everything. I just go back to my classroom and shut the door.

MR. HOURS: The thing about the Puerto Ricans is they think they're one big family. I mean, I think it's nice, I do. It's just sometimes they're not as professional as they should be. I mean having their kids come with them to school, the women laughing and talking so loud in Spanish. They all sticking together, especially at lunch. The women, especially, have like a little colony.

MRS. WEST: It's like all of them [Puerto Rican teachers] are related to each other. But sometimes the noise, because it's a loud culture, just forces us into our rooms [classrooms], just to get some peace and quiet, you know? It's like part of the culture. I mean, some of them, the women, can be perfectly nice.

For these white teachers, places such as the school lunchroom are thought to be "taken over" by the faculty of Puerto Rican descent. In the view of the white faculty, as the Puerto Rican teachers "stick together" and "speak loudly" in Spanish, they are being forced to retreat into their classrooms. Although the white females tend to qualify their statements by saying something "nice," they still participate in a sustained racist discourse. Feeling "excluded," Mr. Hours describes the women of Puerto Rican descent as creating a "colony" in the lunchroom. During my observations, on occasion I would hear white teachers make reference to similar notions. For example, one day in the faculty cafeteria, Mrs. Diaz was using the microwave oven to heat up her lunch which she brought in from home. While Mr. Perry was walking into the cafeteria to get some coffee, he said, "Smells like little Puerto Rico in here. . . . I don't know how you guys [Puerto Rican women at table] can eat that stuff; it smells terrible."

By focusing on how this institution is being "taken over" and how they are being "forced out," these white teachers assume that the school was theirs to begin with. With these strict separatist racial spheres and attitudes observed, for example, in the morning before class, in the faculty lounge, and at lunch, it can be argued that the bilingual institution encourages divisions along racial lines which support the notion of white dominance. In denigrating those faculty of Puerto Rican descent while scripting their own behavior as acceptable, these white teachers are active maintainers of the structural advantages of race privilege. The various ways the white faculty go about constructing an otherwise unmarked location of whiteness all involve placing "others" at their borders. As many contend (Woodson, 1933; Frankenberg, 1993), those who are white often lack an awareness of how their racial positions are constructed in relation to those from oppressed groups. In other words, in order for white people to understand who they are in racial terms, they have to know who they are not. By assigning negative attributes to the Puerto Rican faculty, these white teachers seemingly prop up their own sense of white superiority.

While tension between faculty and the principal obviate in relation to what teachers view as Mrs. Martin's distrust in their abilities and her tendency not to treat them as professionals, issues of race also emerge as they discuss her hire. As discerned from their narrations, some of the Puerto Rican teachers say they are still upset that a Spanish-speaking Puerto Rican administrator was not appointed to the position of principal. After Mrs. Martin was hired, a group of Puerto Rican teachers reportedly complained to the Board of Education that the new principal did not speak Spanish. Their argument was that since some students only speak Spanish, the selected principal would not be able to effectively communicate with them. The outcome of these complaints, as told by Mrs. Martin and the white teachers I interviewed, was the hire of a Spanish-speaking Puerto Rican assistant to the principal, Mrs. Delgato. The white teachers, however, have their own set of complaints about the creation of Mrs. Delgato's position, which some view as favoring Puerto Ricans.

> MR. HOURS: They [Board of Education] are in dire financial straits, yet they have the money to create a brand-new position? When white people complain, nothing is done about their problems. But when somebody else around here complains, the situation somehow gets fixed.

> MR. PERRY: I've got nothing against Anna Delgato. It's just that she was hired under circumstances that were not exactly on the up and up. It's, like, unheard of to create a new job these days. . . . Now they're [Board of Education] paying two salaries. Then they cut aides [teacher aides] to deserving teachers.

> MRS. STEFANSKI: I don't mean anything racial about it, but it does seem when the Puerto Rican faculty ask for things, they get them. It just seems so incredulous to me that when some of the bilingual teachers were angry they weren't getting a Puerto Rican principal, they complained and then were made happy. . . . I know I shouldn't be saying this, but it seems minorities in general are kind of kept happy in this system.

These white teachers contend that "minorities" are being catered to by the Board of Education, at the expense of those who are white.

Puerto Rican faculty members and the African American principal are viewed as unfairly banding together and ganging up on white faculty. In their opinion, the complaints of white teachers are not listened to, while the issues the faculty of Puerto Rican descent raise are resolved in sometimes less than circumspect ways. Again, these white teachers draw a line between "minorities" and themselves, constructing their white selves as morally just and as the voice of reason. It is worth noting that in some ways, it is likely debatable whether the Puerto Rican teachers consider they got what they wanted from the school board.

The narrations of the faculty at the bilingual school also indicate that racial spheres between white and Puerto Rican teachers are further maintained by controversy over the assigning of teacher aides. Many white teachers contend the Spanish track teachers are being favored by the principal in that all of the aides are assigned to only their classes. The Spanish track teachers, however, conclude they deserve the extra help because they have more work to do, as they have to teach in Spanish, back up everything in English, and stop to handle comprehension problems. As mentioned, some of the white teachers bypassed Mrs. Martin and complained to the Board of Education about this situation, which they believed to be unfair. In the final analysis, the board left the problem up to the principal to decide.

> MR. PEAK: What they [administrators] should do is split the aides' time down the middle, fifty–fifty. That's the only way it's going to be fair. . . . What they're doing now is blatant discrimination. My time is just as valuable as the other teachers'.

> MRS. WEST: I hear their [Puerto Rican teachers] arguments, but it's still not right. We all have busy lives and a lot going on. Since there are not that many aides to go around, Mrs. Martin should, like, rotate them in a way that everyone gets help at one time or another. It would be so nice if someone could help me check in homework once in a while. . . . I just feel like there's a lot of favoritism around here.

> MR. HOWELL: The board obviously considers the time and efforts of some teachers more valuable and important than others. I just want to get them [school board] to understand that, look, I'm a really busy teacher who's trying to give it my all in class. In a lot of ways, I don't think anyone should be given more of a break just because they're from a minority group.

These white teachers view the aides' assignments in the bilingual school as based on favoritism for Puerto Rican teachers. When Mr. Peak exclaims, "The minorities are given things just because of their race," and when Mr. Howell, a seventh grade math teacher, says, "I don't think anyone should be given more of a break just because they're from a minority group," they include all who are not white in their complaint. In their logic, "minorities" look out for "minorities," while those who are white suffer. Again, these comments do not necessarily reflect the views of all of the white teachers, yet they exemplify some of the racist ideology that is currently active in the school. This discourse likely plays a significant part in shaping racialized spheres, and, therefore, daily relations among the principal, teachers, and students at the school.

Separatist gender/race spheres are produced in the bilingual school, which arguably contribute to the sexism and racism that has been narrated and enacted by the Canal Town girls and boys, setting up those of Puerto Rican and African descent as "other" in the dialectical production of white adolescent identity. Although the distribution of such messages is likely not deliberate, the polorization among teachers along gender and racial lines in terms of seating patterns, school policies, and the occasional overt remark is hard to ignore. In this school, as the male teachers freely enter and exit "female" space, the white boys are additionally encouraged to position white females as "other," therefore, abetting the historical white tradition of male dominance. The tendency of some white teachers to complain that "minorities" are treated better by the school board potentially emboldens the discourse of lost entitlement among white young men.

Identity among Canal Town females emerges in respect to that of the constructed white male identity and in relation to that of the male and female "other." While white and Puerto Rican female faculty complain as a group that they are expected to do extra jobs, potential gender challenges are minimal, and do not include a critique of inequity between women and men that extends outside into the broader world. The school seemingly does not inspirit girls to criticize gender roles, which is significant, because even though the white Canal Town females narrate lives that are saturated with domestic violence, they view such abuse as normal. By not addressing the issue of domestic violence on any level, the school must be seen as participating in the silencing of this social epidemic. By ignoring the issue of abuse, the boys, who exhibited tendencies toward abusive behavior, do not learn that this is wrong.

As their narrations indicate, the Canal Town girls have plans for the future which include graduating from college and living as single, financially and emotionally independent career women. By envisioning adulthood in such a way, these girls intend to spare themselves from the abuse that presently inscribes their lives and their mothers'. In the bilingual school, however, students are not being prepared with the critical and analytical skills needed to score high enough on college entrance exams to gain admission. Teachers, in fact, admit they do not imagine their students will really go on to college. Although they are telling youth about the importance of higher education in landing a good job, they are not preparing them to achieve this end. In this sense, the school is also contributing to schooling females who in the future will be unprepared to compete for jobs that will allow them financial independence. Many of these females, therefore, will be forced back into violent homes. In school, the white Canal Town girls and boys are being encouraged to reproduce the conditions of their lives—conditions that are never historically contextualized in the current economy.

The very nature of the school being bilingual ostensibly encourages cultural understanding and exchange. White and Puerto Rican female faculty did rally around what they thought were points of gender inequality within the school, and these instances of coming together can be seen as related to the tendencies within female Canal Town identity. Although the white Canal Town girls evidence an emerging sense of racism, as compared to their white male peers, they say they make a few acquaintances across cultures. Still, these attempts are minimal, and for the most part, the bilingual school can be said to perpetuate divisions along gender/race lines. Involved in a pattern of control over teacher labor, the principal promotes the importance of the form of material, rather than content. This accentuation on form shapes the way knowledge is distributed by teachers, which ultimately also contributes to the contradictory attitudes toward schooling and knowledge seen among the Canal Town girls and boys. It seems that nowhere at this school will these youth learn the skills needed to view their realities as socially constructed. By not engaging them in meaningful critique, the school, then, does not disrupt the tendency among these young females and males to blame "others."

Although the white teachers are not from Canal Town, they articulate sentiments about feeling devalued and pushed into stifling, rapidly shrinking spaces, which parallel the complaints of Canal Town youth. Inside the bilingual institution, which they characterize as having been "taken over" by "minorities," the white teachers and youth say they have very few spaces to go where they can feel refreshed and reinvigorated. Living in historically working class urban white communities, mostly north of Canal Town, all of the white teachers narrate family histories in which they, their fathers, and their grandfathers labored in the industrial plants near the canal. As the white teachers and Canal Town youth narrate a similar discourse of being continuously under siege inside the school, a white working class protectionist language emerges that is not just trapped within the confines of Canal Town, but is seemingly fused to larger social movements directed against affirmative action, anti-immigration, and welfare reform. In the next chapter, it will be seen that the poor white Canal Town youth turn to the Center for relief, as it is a space in which they feel they belong and are considered important. Compared to the school, the Center is a location in which these youth can freely assert their race, ethnic, class, and gender locations.

CHAPTER 6

The Canal Town Community Center

In this chapter, I explore how the poor white Canal Town youth construct identities in the space of the neighborhood community center. In describing how, through relationships formed with certain staff members, all of whom are white, and through participation in favorite activities, such as Girls' Club and structured recreation in the gym, both the girls and boys set up the Center as an alternative site to what they feel are unwelcoming homes, dangerous streets, and an unresponsive school. While the notion of "free space" (Evans & Boyte, 1992) is seemingly useful in understanding how individuals work toward a sense of belonging and shaping collective political goals, it does not account for the type of hegemonic and oppressive objectives that are actually produced at the Center. Evans and Boyte, furthermore, do not provide a model for interrogating spaces organized by adults for youth. In this corner of the Canal Town community, adults are distributing displaced messages about economic dispossession to the children who attend, and are encouraging them to take part in political projects. As racist community ideology is elaborated upon and transmitted transgenerationally, the Canal Town youth are learning to imagine the future through narrow vistas.

Similar to "free space" (Evans & Boyte, 1992), the Center exists in a place between private lives and institutions, where individuals get together and critically assess their surroundings with the goal of change. The Center is a highly political setting, in which ordinary people are not just complaining about their plight, but are developing public skills, valuing civic cooperation, and constructing a strong group identity. In this space, employees creatively shore up goals by making group decisions as they work toward solving the problems they see facing area youth. For example, by gathering student report cards, staff members decided that attending youth needed to raise their grades; thus, they planned a structured homework program. In an attempt to "clean up" their streets, other employees organized block club meetings.

In order for employees to sustain the role they create for the Center—as a place in which white youth can grow into what they determine as healthy and responsible adults—these staff extend outside the facility to forge relationships with other institutions of social life. In this way, the Center has been successful in developing a strong support network that enhances efforts to get things done. To this end, similar to "free space" (Evans & Boyte, 1992), employees are making linkages to broader patterns of decision making, social life, and institutional practice. The director of the Center seemingly networks with diverse groups of people, such as business representatives, politicians, and leaders of other neighborhood organizations. This way, when there is a fund-raising drive or when some kind of favor is needed, the director can draw upon the resources of local corporations and politicians. By maintaining connections with other community centers, these organizations have successfully lobbied together to demand change.

Upon closer examination of the Center as a "free space," however, it actually is less a space that is "free," and more a space that is narrowly conceived. The public participation on behalf of Canal Town staff, youth, and senior citizens can be seen as motivated by feelings of superiority over those of African and Puerto Rican descent. Particularly the employees, who are supported by their community, are acting upon resistance and reaction to changes they believe those from culturally oppressed groups are bringing into their neighborhood and school. These individuals believe if they do not step in to provide a nurturing environment for white local youth, "minorities" will take over. In choosing those external organizations with which to network to reach goals, there is arguably no intentional inclusion of voices that might pose personal/political opposition. As leaders of select organizations are invited inside the Center to help make decisions, ideology is never seriously challenged. Due to this fact, in terms of race, norms of egalitarian exchange, debate, dissent, and openness, for the most part, do not prevail. Inside this space—which is sustained by carefully guarded white networks—white Canal Town youth partake in services and help to keep the Center in operation.

It is within this context that the Canal Town youth turn to the Center as an escape from their troubles. Against a backdrop in which racism, poverty, violence, and concealment of abuse at home and school blend in the lives of Canal Town girls, these females characterize the Center as a safe hideout from all that is so wrong. The girls value as important their relationship with Ruby, the white elderly activities coordinator, whom they view as a mother-like figure and friend. Compared to school, where they feel Puerto Rican students are favored by teachers, in the white space of the Center, the girls participate in a muted form of racism. In the Center, and in particular, Girls' Club, these white females feel a strong sense of belonging. Although forums such as Girls' Club do exist in which these youth *could* potentially learn to speak out about racism and the violence which they endure in their lives, as they are not taught otherwise, they continue to deal with their abuse alone.

As they reflect on life at home, on the streets, and in school, the Canal Town boys have thus far exhibited sexist and racist tendencies, as well as their potential as present and future victimizers of white females and males from culturally oppressed groups. As they characterize the Center, however, the white boys say they value the sense of family and belonging they feel when they attend. In particular, they claim the gym as their own, and they work to maintain it as an all-male, all-white space. Their inclination to patrol the borders of the gymnasium floor at the Center can be seen in response to anger over the belief that those of Puerto Rican descent have "taken over" the school, which seemingly threatens their felt sense of privilege. Inside the gym at the Center, the boys continue to narrate the language of lost entitlement to public funds and grant money. Although forums do exist inside the Center in which boys *could* learn to critique their violently sexist, racist, and, as will be seen, homophobic attitudes, such thinking is not interrupted.

THE CENTER

As explained by Felicia, the director of the Center, in the late 1950s, a group of concerned Canal Town residents met in a home where the Center now stands in order to discuss ways to prevent the rise in neighborhood crime. The group decided to focus on ways to provide recreation for area youth. Under the leadership of a few dedicated residents, contends Felicia, the association became incorporated in 1960. With the donation of a warehouse near the docks, and through the fund-raising and organization skills of volunteers, the space opened as a community center. As the makeshift community center was instantly popular with local youth, Felicia recalls that the association soon began to lobby for the building of a bigger space, and in 1965, the city donated money for the construction and maintenance of the present-day community center in Canal Town.

Opening in 1967, the new facility featured a large gymnasium, an indoor swimming pool, equipment storage rooms, and a few small offices. Early programs at the Center, such as arts and crafts and open recreation in the gym, were geared toward children, teenagers, and young adults. The only neighborhood newsletter in the city, the *Canal Town News*, also began operation out of the offices of the Center during this time, and continues in circulation today. In 1970, the Evanston meat-packing plant rented space from the community center, a relationship which continues to this day.

Felicia says that in 1990, she took the job as director over from Carolyn, one of the elderly former Canal Town residents interviewed for this project, who held the position since the beginning. Felicia's hire was successfully recommended to the city by the board of directors of the Center, which continues to consist of lifelong Canal Town residents, most of whom are senior citizens. Needing more resources to support expanding services, in 1990, supported by the board of directors, Felicia tells how she negotiated with the city to take control over the Center. The city obliged, agreeing to continue to maintain the building, while a public granting agency pledged ongoing funding, allowing the Center to take on the job of programming, supplies, and staffing. In the early 1990s, a large meeting room with tables, several offices, a kitchen, and a food pantry— was built onto the existing Center, doubling it in size. Today the Canal Town youth use this space for homework, for eating dinner and snacks, and for activities such as Girls' Club and Boys' Club.

At present, the Center is open from 11:00 A.M. until 10:00 P.M. Monday through Saturday, and, as mentioned earlier, is typically patronized by two groups of Canal Town residents: youth and senior citizens. Although workshops on parenting and job development aimed toward adults are held at the Center, practically no one attends. Senior citizens come to the Center in the morning, where they play cards, eat lunch, and work on crafts. These visitors stay until the youth arrive from school. As soon as school lets out, all of the youth who attend walk over directly from school, including the eighteen participants in this study. Felicia tells me that about two hundred local youth are in regular attendance at the Center. Among this group, says Felicia, all are enrolled in the bilingual school, all are from the community, and about 85 percent are white, while 15 percent are of Puerto Rican descent. Felicia also reports that the white kids are more or less evenly divided along gender lines, while only Puerto Rican girls attend (Grant Agency Demographics, 1996). Upon coming from school, the kids typically have a snack. The boys then head into the gym and the girls talk to Ruby, do their homework, read books, or do some artwork. Throughout the week, there is a regular calendar of activities during the evening for these youth. The gym is closed on Mondays because it is food pantry distribution night; Tuesday nights are for Boys' Club; Wednesday nights are for Girls' Club; Thursday nights are workshops for parents; and Friday nights are for open swim and swimming lessons, which is followed by a fun activity, such as a dance or recreation. Sports leagues run throughout the week.

STAFF

McLaughlin, Irby, and Langman (1994) identify successful leaders of organizations for urban youth as those who create spaces in which children can imagine productive futures despite incredible odds. As outlined by these authors, exemplary leaders of organizations for adolescents exhibit a set of similar core qualities, which include, a respect and dedication to youth, a commitment to serve others, and an enthusiasm for their job. At the Canal Town community center, there are three full-time and three part-time employees, as mentioned, all whom are white. As will be heard in the narrations of the Canal Town girls and boys, the three full-time staff— Felicia, the director; Ruby, the programs coordinator; and, Mitchell, the recreation coordinator—have seemingly gained their implicit trust. The part-time employees—the accountant, the administrative assistant, and the swimming instructor/lifeguard—have jobs which restrict their interaction with patrons, and for at least this reason, may not be identified by area youth as crucial figures in their lives. All employees, however, were born and raised in Canal Town, and have long family histories in that area of the city. Felicia, Ruby, and Mitchell emphasize their historical investments in the neighborhood.

FELICIA: I spent my whole life in Canal Town. My father was born on Hydrolic Avenue. He was a longshoreman. His grandfather helped dig the canal. They were from Ireland. Actually, for a while my grandfather ran a rag business, horse and wagon kind of thing for money. He ran it out of the house until he died. . . . I live in that same house now. I'll be like him [grandfather], never moving off the street. My mother's father was from Canal Town too, Irish Catholics going back many generations, old canal diggers. This is an Irish neighborhood and a lot of the waterfront [dock workers] and steel people settled here.

RUBY: I was born and raised here [Canal Town]. [I was] Born on Lock Street, number 212, raised at 176 and 178, and now I live at 166. So I've spent my entire life on Lock Street . . . my mom and dad were from here. My father's people date back to the Civil War. My great-grandfather on my father's side came from Ireland, got a job digging the canal, wound up in Canal Town, and then left to fight. I actually have the old musket that was the one my great-grandfather used in the war. I use it to poke around the ashes in the stove [wood-burning stove]. Yes, my family is one of the oldest Irish Catholic families.

MITCHELL: My family lines go way back. They came on my farther's and mother's sides from Ireland. Catholic canal men on both sides, ended up in Canal Town. . . . My great-grandfather got in a fight one night when he was drunk, and they found him the next morning, drowned in the canal. My great-grandmother was left with ten kids to raise on her own . . . she survived by having her kids sell corned beef sandwiches to the men up and down the docks. The canal supported my family for generations. Because of the help of the likes of my family, this city opened up; hell, the West opened up.

As the quotes indicate, Felicia, Ruby, and Mitchell have strong historical connections to Canal Town. For these three employees, this is a point of pride, and Ruby and Mitchell emphasize their ancestors' roles in participating in what they isolate as major historical events, such as fighting in the Civil War and helping to "open up" the Western part of the country. Mitchell also describes what he believes to be a reciprocal relationship that Irish workers had with the canal. In his view, the Irish worked on the canal, while the canal continued to provide them with a livelihood. Felicia, Ruby, and Mitchell imply they are intimately connected to the neighborhood in a way that no outsider could duplicate. In fact, Felicia explains to me that in selecting staff, it is requisite that candidates be qualified *and* longtime residents, "so they are a part of the neighborhood, so they will come in knowing the children's problems real well because they've lived side-by-side with the families."

These three employees all make reference to their Irish Catholic ancestry, and as the earlier narrations of the elderly Canal Town residents indicate, they appear to well represent the ethnic and religious heritage of the neighborhood. Being Irish American and Catholic is a commonality among all those who work at the Center, and as Felicia tells me, it has always been that way. To this end, the history of Irish American Catholics in the United States perhaps becomes bound up in what constitutes the norms at the Center, including how things are run and which kids are allowed inside. As some authors explain (Roediger, 1994; Ignatiev, 1995), Irish Catholics who came to the United States in the eighteenth and nineteenth centuries were escaping lives as impoverished peasants at the hands of Protestant landlords. Upon arrival, the Irish people found that color was an extreme indication of social status—a situation they arguably did not have to deal with as much in Ireland due to the homogeneity of rural life. Irish workers were considered one step up in acceptability from enslaved Africans, and therefore found only menial jobs such as digging canals and railroad beds. In producing a sense of self as superior, in some cases, those Irish immigrants exuberantly participated in rendering those of African descent into a racialized substatus group. The use by capital of Black labor to break strikes also fueled racist attitudes among Irish American workers (Roediger, 1991). As Felicia, Ruby, and Mitchell describe their ancestors as coming from Ireland to the United States to work on the canal, it is worth considering the extent to which such historical tendencies among that ethnic group are potentially maintained today at the Center.

The three full-time employees at the Center have varied backrounds. Felicia, who is young, married, and has three small children, as mentioned in a previous chapter, is the only community center employee to go on to higher education. She obtained her BS in nursing from the local state college in 1988. Her husband is from Canal Town and works on the line at a Chevy plant. Felicia's mother watches her pre-school children dring the day while she works at the Center. Felicia is of the opinion that her educational background "legitimates" her in the eyes of the staff, community, and funding sources. Ruby is an elderly, unmarried high schol graduate. Mitchell is 65, and is married with six grown children. Mitchell graduated from the ninth grade, and then, as he reports, spent over ten years abusing drugs, until he finally got into a rehabilitation program. Mitchell recounts how upon completion of the program, Carolyn promised him a job if he stayed clean. Ruby and Mitchell attended the Canal Town bilingual school back in the days before it was transformed into a bilingual institution. When asked to describe what they do at the Center today, Felicia, Ruby, and Mitchell explain specific tasks while at the same time revealing that they have emotional attachments to the population of youth they serve.

> FELICIA: The main thing I do is grant writing. One of the burdens I have that is not shared by most directors is the operations of the building. The repairs and getting in touch with the city when things need to be repaid, fixing the pool. . . . I pretty much have an open door policy. My door is never closed, unless I have a grant due by 4:00 [P.M.] and it's noon. The kids pretty much wander in to talk. As you can see, I'm buried in paperwork and deadlines and things. It's a lot of work for just a few staff. I mean we have no janitor. So the kids and the staff are responsible for everything, wiping up the floors in the bathroom, everything. . . . It's not a job, it's a lifestyle. . . . I learned a lot from Carolyn about using the Center as a way to keep the neighborhood sane. I want our kids to achieve; that, to me, is success . . .

> RUBY: Well, basically I set up programming, alternate activities for the children so they're not out on the streets . . . I develop programming, and have trainings every week so that they could get educated in areas of drugs and sexually transmitted diseases, and traffic safety, everything. But as the program evolved and as we all grew, we became a family, you know? That's part of my problem, it's not a job anymore, it's my family . . . you get involved, you get emotionally involved. You feel like a parent to all these kids. It's hard, because you love them. Actually that's the easy part, loving them. It's watching them do things that are hurting themselves that's hard. That really grips you, and then, you know, you lose your night's sleep and stuff over it.

> MITCHELL: I coach all the sports here. We've got boys' baseball, basketball, hockey, and football. We've got the little kids' team, then kids from the middle school. We have girls' teams but most of the time no girls show up. . . . I let the boys practice in the gym when this happens . . . so really, it's pretty much only boys in the gym. . . . But the

real, most important thing I do here is look after the kids, make sure when they have problems that someone cares. I don't care what time of day it is, morning, noon, or night . . . if they need me, I'm there. They just need an adult to talk to. . . . There are very few fathers in this neighborhood who act like fathers, so I try to be a good role model for them.

These employees demonstrate they are deeply concerned with the lives of participating youth, and they do not look at their work as bounded by the actual hours spent on the clock. Felicia relays how her main job is to research and write grants, carry out assessments, and submit and resubmit for funding. She also characterizes her work as a "lifestyle," and measures her own success by the future of the participating youth. As Ruby explains her objectives for programming activities, she maintains that through the years she has come to assume a parent role. It is hard for her, Ruby reveals, when kids do things that hurt themselves, and she worries about the local youth even when she is at home. Mitchell reports he coaches and organizes recreational leagues, yet he considers making sure the kids have a father figure with whom they can talk as his most important job. Felicia, Ruby, and Mitchell all make allusions to "family" in detailing their work with Canal Town youth. When asked to describe the children who visit the Center, Felicia, Ruby, and Mitchell characterize them as good kids who have a lot of problems as a result of troubling conditions in their lives.

FELICIA: We've got all types of kids here. There are kids from one-parent homes, some live with their grandparents, but basically they're all good kids, from the old Irish families. They may get into occasional trouble and are mischievous, but they're good-hearted kids. They want to feel like they're part of something, like they're doing something. They just want to be part of something. . . . They don't at home. Even when you call and ask the parents to come down they very rarely do. The kids are here, and as Ruby will tell you, we can hold them until they're in their early teens. It's just like a family. . . . Parents are not doing what they're supposed to be doing. They're not spending time with their kids. They don't come to any of the functions and many are in trouble with the law. It's frustrating. They're in and out of jail. Also, the streets are full of drugs, violence, crime, brought in by minorities. Another thing, at the school, our kids are not learning English. We're accommodating to them [Puerto Ricans] and we also got to speak Spanish to them? The white kids are the ones who suffer. The kids and teachers from Puerto Rico, they just pick up and go from months on end back home. The school, as far as I can see, is the main thing that's failing our kids. . . . The Spanish that are coming here [to the Center] are good. They speak English; they always are the first kids to volunteer to help out, clean the bathrooms, whatever. The ones [Puerto Rican youth] from the east side that are shipped in to the school here [neighborhood] are rough; the Spanish kids here at the Center shy away from that. . . . There's some bad ones [Puerto Rican youth] right in this neighborhood. They know better than to try to step foot inside.

RUBY: They're all the same. They really are. Good kids from families that have been here for years. The girls try to seek attention anywhere they can get it, even if it's with boys in the fields. In one way, the girls come, I would say, to be near the boys, but it's not the real reason. When they get in here on Girls' Club night, they're over here by themselves and they do their own thing. All of them act like little girls then, even the older ones. You see, these kids didn't have much of a childhood, with all the drugs at home. . . . The neighborhood is so really dangerous now, with minorities moving in, bringing in trouble . . . our kids don't have much of a chance out there. . . . Girls' Club is someplace to go where you can forget all that. . . . Even my Spanish girls come. I still don't know all their names, but they don't mind. I just can't tell them apart . . . I accept them [Puerto Rican girls] though. . . . The ones here [Puerto Rican girls] are the ones who are not in trouble. No Puerto Rican boys come to the Center though. . . . Most of the kids who come here, if they weren't here they'd be hanging on the corner or in a warehouse someplace and getting into trouble that they shouldn't be into. They don't want to go home, so this is the only safe place to go. . . . Their parents don't have dreams so the kids don't have dreams. There's no supervision in the home . . . it's now mother and boyfriend, or mother and uncle . . . the fathers, they're transients. They're wherever. If they're there, they're not involved. And they just don't care. . . . The mothers are too busy . . . it could be a new man in their life, drugs, alcohol. . . . So we [at the Center] become the babysitting service. You know. They [parents] feel their kids are here and the adults here will supervise them. But they don't realize their kids ain't always here. And that's where the problems begin. . . . The school favors minority children. Those children are getting the advantages, so we [at the Center] have to pickup the slack.

MITCHELL: Basically, they're all good kids. . . . I really work with groups of boys. They're great kids, and great athletes. . . . The girls that come here are on the brink of trouble. They're experimenting with things they shouldn't. Marijuana, sex, alcohol. . . . They just cut through the gym while the guys are practicing. . . . If we had the church and school working with us, it would be ideal. . . . The school just cares about the minorities . . . it makes me so mad. . . . Even we [at the Center] only get City Hall to maintain the building only because of the minorities here. If it was only white [people] here, we'd get squat. . . . The streets around here are getting bad, not like when I was a boy. You had your friends back then, and there'd be fights, but it was harmless. Today you got your Blacks and Puerto Ricans coming in bringing big time trouble.

The community center staff see the institutions that structure the lives of area youth as failing them. Felicia and Ruby are critical of parents, whom they view as neglecting their children and involved in unlawful activity. Despite their assertions of child neglect and drug abuse in white homes, all three employees, however, also point to "minorities" whom they believe are taking over neighborhood streets and making them unsafe. Each individual is also angry at the school, which they believe is ignoring the needs of white youth and putting the concerns of "minorities" first. Ruby reveals that because of this, it is up to the Center to "pick up the slack" for the white kids.

For Felicia, Ruby, and George, the "good" kid is seemingly white and from an old Irish American Canal Town family. Although most "minorities" are characterized as deviant, Felicia makes distinctions between the "good" Puerto Rican females who come to the Center, speak English, and help out, and those who are Spanish-speaking and "rough." According to these narrations, males of Puerto Rican descent are thought of as dangerous, and are suspiciously not in attendance at the Center. Ruby talks about "her Spanish girls" who come to Girls' Club. Even though she cannot "tell them apart," she says she "accepts" them. Ruby's distinction between types of Puerto Ricans resembles the views of the Canal Town girls.

Mitchell, on the other hand, is incensed over the "Blacks and Puerto Ricans" who he views as involved in street violence and ruining things in the community and school for the kids he works closest with—white boys. In Mitchell's view, City Hall is responsive to the Center only because "minorities" are in attendance. This thinking is reflective of the same sentiments seen among Canal Town boys and white male teachers. Additionally worth noting, Mitchell is angry at girls at the Center who cut through the gym, which he describes as the domain of the white boys. Still, Felicia, Ruby, and Mitchell contend that the Center plays an extremely important role in the lives of white Canal Town youth.

FELICIA: This community center is unique and I try to tell the State this too. They keep talking about program funding and outcome funding and that's fine; I can see that. . . . I keep telling them we have a lot of social events, to make people feel a part of it [the Center] and to recruit volunteers. We do a lot of fun things. They [State] don't really see that as priority programming. They don't see the value in it. So I've been trying to stress that I think our Center is unique because the kids don't come here and stay for only an hour because they've received a service or participated in a program. They come here the whole day and maybe partake of a program, but they're here for the entire day and they're eating meals, doing homework, playing sports, talking out their problems with staff, helping to take care of the place, taking swimming lessons, or whatever. That's why I make sure I'm out there and seen in the city. That's why I network. I want to be able to afford the extra things that make this place like a home . . . you know, buying snacks for the kids, extra hats and mittens in the winter; it's not in the State budget. Only the bare minimum is there. There's so much to do. I work closely with the directors at north side [community center] and the Riley Road Center. We [directors] share ideas for funding, are in the same sports leagues, we even lobby together against City Hall when one of us has a big need that is being neglected. . . . I buy tickets to all the events in the city. I get dressed up and I go. I mingle with people, give them my card, tell them about the Center. . . . Then when I need help raising money, people remember us.

RUBY: The Center, it's their [area youth] life. This is what their life surrounds. They come home from school, only they don't go home. They come here. This is their home. They eat here, they play here, they socialize here. They get taught here. They do their homework here. They play in the gym here. Everything is this community center. Everything . . . there's nothing for them [area youth] to go home to after school. What are they going home to? Mom is usually drunk or high, or Dad, or uncle, older sister, brother, whoever. And there's nothing for them at home, but yelling, and screaming, and fighting, and arguing, and more drugs and more problems. . . . The kids here, the little ones, age 4 and 5, they leave [the Center] at ten o'clock, walk home by themselves in the dark. . . . Some don't want to go home. They beg you to keep the place open. But we can't. First of all, we can't because financially we can't keep it open. They [children] beg me to; I used to have sleepovers but I'd be wiped out because I'd have to stay up all night to watch them, you know? But I have late nights with them. I stay here at the Center and take care of the kids. . . . Felicia goes out into the city. Felicia has raised quite a bit of money for this center. She's very good at that. It's as much who you know as what you know. She writes nice grants. She presents them well. It's politics, and you've got to go where the money comes from. She makes sure they know about us. She attends functions like three, four times a week. She works a ninety-hour week. Without Felicia, our family here would fall apart . . . without the money she brings in to give our children what they're not given at home and school, our children would fall through the cracks.

MITCHELL: The Center is everything to the boys. They're really learning to be great athletes . . . they learn sportsmanship, how to work as a team. They even organize their own practices. . . . They're lucky they got almost, like, their own gym and equipment to practice with. . . . I'll tell you, we're [staff] all trying to keep this place good. Felicia goes out and gets money. A lot of people are worried the Center will go downhill like the neighborhood, where certain people are bringing in drugs and violence . . . it's like mostly minorities that do this. So to protect the neighborhood and the Center, Felicia got a

grant last year for me and a local police officer to organize block
clubs. We're going to get the older boys' sports team [white Canal
Town boys] involved. We're going to organize and make sure this
neighborhood doesn't go downhill any more.

According to Felicia, her primary funding source does not understand that the Center is much more than an occasional provider of services in the lives of area youth. Instead, Felicia views the facility as a
family, and a place where youth can go to feel needed. Ruby and
Mitchell also think of the Center as a home. But in order to secure the
resources it takes to maintain a home-like quality, Felicia's efforts to
raise money outside the walls of the building are seen by her and the
other employees as central.

This theme of reaching outside the Center to other neighborhood
organizations, businesses, and politicians is a strong current as Felicia
describes her work. For instance, as Felicia explains, it is important to
diversify funding and reliance upon operation services through networking with politicians and by making corporate connections. Felicia
claims she has worked hard to forge connections with every business in
the area, so now when there is a fundraising campaign, or when a service is needed, she is a lot more successful. For example, says Felicia,
once she obtained a grant from the city to replace the swimming pool
filter, and the city did not have anyone to haul out the old one. Felicia
states she simply called Illinois Chem, a chemical company in the neighborhood, and they sent over a group of engineers to dismantle the old
filter and haul it away, pro bono. In the past year alone, Illinois Chem
has donated $5,000 to the recreation center. Efforts, therefore, are made
on behalf of the Center to obtain the support needed to maintain and
strengthen a particular set of interactions among patrons.

Felicia explains it is vital to keep up good relations with funding
sources. For instance, she tries when she can to have the Center provide
services for the donating industry. One spring, a desire among the local
chemical industry was the formation of some sort of recreational league.
The Canal Town community center responded by creating the "Industrial Softball League" of thirteen teams—a league that still exists today.
Felicia also makes sure she is backed by the Canal Town community by
showing support for local concerns.

In other instances, connections are specifically made with neighbor-
ing white, Irish, similarly thinking centers in order to raise a voice to
"lobby" for change. For instance, Felicia explains that a few years ago,
the north side community center did not have a gymnasium, and even
though the building was exclusively under city control, the director had
been unsuccessful in trying to attract the City's attention to this need.

Felicia says she and the director at North Side and Riley Road called a meeting with the city council persons from each district, and formed, she says, "a sort of consortium" through which they successfully argued their case. Three years later, the new gym was in operation.

It is not the construction of the gym that is problematic, but the fact that only those community centers in historically white neighborhoods serving primarily white residents are banding together to create goals and to be heard. As the Canal Town Center employees see it as their role to counteract the "minority favoritism" they believe to be experienced by area white youth in the school, by joining forces with other white Irish American centers, they can ensure that their agendas are fulfilled. It is important to note it is not just the directors of these agencies that are the energy behind these organizing forces. As Mitchell relays, he works with the police, and, he hopes, the Canal Town boys, to build up block clubs. With these block clubs, Mitchell hopes to patrol the neighborhood and the Center from a "minority" presence. In fact, Felicia, Ruby, and Mitchell reveal that the connections made outside the Center are often motivated by racism.

FELICIA: There's a lot of transient people moving in, most of them Hispanic. Even though they don't own the property, they should respect the property. There's this house on Hydrolic Avenue, that upstairs has a family of fifteen, downstairs has a family of ten. It's a mess. The Hispanic in this neighborhood pretty much live in disarray, and it's accepted among their own. Some of them are ignorant and just don't know any better. It's cultural. So we're going to work together with North Side and Riley [community centers] to try to introduce them to some kind of training. They [Puerto Rican residents] really don't know they're doing something that's not accepted by the rest of the people. That's why they'd probably be better off on the west side. . . . They're some [Puerto Ricans] that are dirt poor, but as little as you have, you can always afford to be clean. There's no excuse for that.

RUBY: What also used to be a part of Canal Town is where the Pepper Projects are now. Back in the 1950s and 1960s they [the City] ripped a lot of housing out to make way for the Pepper Projects. That was the start of the downfall of this neighborhood because it brought in people from outside the neighborhood, like Blacks, and it has been downhill ever since. After that Hispanics started moving in. I don't think the City realizes when they do things like that how badly they disrupt a neighborhood. . . . They don't ask people in the neighborhood for their opinions. The other problem the community had is when the projects went up, some long-standing people moved out. They didn't sell their houses, but started renting them out. And after a while they didn't watch their property. The tenants they get are mostly minorities and such. It's driving good people out, and more minorities in. That's the other thing. Were always trying to get on top of the people that own property that are renting. They need to be made aware of what their property is looking like. We've got Illinois Chem backing us. Somebody has to hold them [African Americans, Puerto Ricans] to a standard. We've got our council person involved. We get the kids to go door to door with petitions. . . . Also, the block clubs Mitchell runs here are trying to keep after the city inspectors. See, if you have a block club and send a letter to the housing authority on club letterhead, you get top priority. Individual calls don't get the attention and priority that block clubs do. Block clubs are a way for people to take control. They have to work to keep it the way it is because nothing is going to hold steady.

MITCHELL: One person complaining about something is not going to get nothing done. Through a community center, if it's an active center, they get a lot done. And that's what's happening here. We're pressuring the housing authority to get people to get the right kind of tenant. . . . We're trying to get the City to work with our Center and with the North Side and Riley Road [community centers]. That's why we have all these neighborhood meetings between centers. We're going to get together and not let the City just turn around and put all the money into something else anymore. For as long as I can remember, Canal Town has been overlooked by the rest of the City. The City is neglecting us, putting money downtown, or into things that are not working. Or they're making questionable decisions, like updating the Pepper Projects. Recently City Hall spent a lot of money on corner brick moldings and fake fronts put on the tops of the tall towers [at the Pepper Projects]. It's crazy. Half the projects are boarded up. Half of them are not being used, and then City Hall turns around and puts all that money into face-lifting? It's absolute nonsense.

Felicia clearly relays that in consortium with other urban white community centers—all to the north of Canal Town—there will be an attempt to help those of Puerto Rican descent overcome what are believed to be deficiencies within the culture. In Felicia's view, and in the opinion of the other directors, those who are Puerto Rican do not know enough to be clean. The comment that those of Puerto Rican descent would likely fit in better on the west side implies that they do not belong in white neighborhoods in the first place. Ruby and Mitchell emphasize the importance of block clubs in cleaning up their neighborhood, which, according to them, has been run over by "minorities." Ruby knows that to get action, you need to be well organized, for example, with letterhead. Ruby also explains how the youth at the Center assist the cause by canvassing the neighborhood with petitions.

Mitchell describes meetings held at the Canal Town community center in which only certain other white Irish American centers were represented to work toward this common goal. And, as Mitchell previously mentioned, he also wants to get the boys involved in these block clubs. Again, these employees overtly evidence that collaborations with other community organizations are sometimes made to maintain white supremacy. As Mitchell contends, "one person complaining about something is not going to get nothing done." If people do not organize to protect themselves, as Ruby states, "nothing is going to hold steady." Interestingly, as mentioned in the previous chapter, five out of the six white teachers who participated in this study live in the area of the city north of Canal Town, and narrate racist discourse that is strikingly similar to that of the Center staff and formerly working class white youth.

On a number of occasions, I heard stories or witnessed accounts of racist behavior on the part of the staff in daily interaction with youth. One day, Felicia was telling me about the problems brought into Canal Town by those of African descent, and stated her belief about "an almost inbred sense to cause trouble that Black kids are raised with." She went on to exemplify her point with a story about "a little Black kid who was in front of the Center and I was trying to shoo him away, and he called me a white bitch! I couldn't believe it! Three years old and he knew that!" Why Felicia was "shooing" the child away, while other young children were allowed to play inside, is not, apparently, an issue at all. In another instance, one day I was in the meeting room talking to Ruby and watching youth read and do their homework. Suddenly, Ruby stopped our conversation midsentence, and began carefully watching an African American boy—rarely seen at the Center—walk into the room, select a book from the children's bookshelf, and sit down to read. A few seconds later, Ruby excused herself, took a set of keys, and locked the pantry door, which was curious, considering this door is always left open. Ruby later told me that she did not want anything "taken." On countless occasions, I heard Mitchell complain that the only reason the Center gets funding is because of the "minorities" who attend, and that "for some reason white people just ain't worth anything." Within this carefully labored upon white space, I now turn to how the white youth go about negotiating identity inside.

GIRLS

As their notion of what the Center means to them unfolds through narrative, it becomes clear that the poor white Canal Town girls position the facility as a retreat from the violence that punctuates their lives at home and on the streets, and the lack of attention they feel they receive at home and school. In response to some of these institutions that structure their lives, the white girls begin to set up the Center—and especially Girls' Club—as a place where they go to feel at ease. In fact, even high school females come to Girls' Club, where they seemingly try to recapture a lost sense of childhood in selecting and participating in activities geared toward little girls. These females highlight as crucial some things they feel are provided in their lives by the Center, which include a sense of belonging, a sense of safety, and a sense that there is interest in their individual well-being.

As the girls feel those from culturally oppressed groups are "invading" their neighborhood and are being unfairly favored in school, the Center becomes a safe white harbor, where those who are white can regain a sense of importance that they feel has systematically been taken away. Although as explained in an earlier chapter, certain Puerto Rican girls do attend the Center, they are not fully accepted into the white girl fold. These young white females participate in a muted form of racism, in that, for example, they only use racial slurs when Puerto Rican girls are not around. The Center, then, contributes in a few ways to shaping white Canal Town female identities—it offers a safe place from domestic abuse *and* a forum in which they can enact group notions of whiteness as superior. When the Canal Town girls are asked to describe what role the Center plays in their lives, it is quite apparent that it is seen as a place of extreme importance:

SALLY: If there was no Center, I would die. I don't know what I would do because this is the one place that I go the most. This is my favorite place in the whole world. I get to meet cute boys. . . . It [the Center] gives me more energy and it makes me not scared of people. It's made me a people person. . . . I was real shy . . . I didn't even talk. I only hung out with little kids. . . . I've been coming here since I was 6. . . . The Center has also been helpful because there's a homework program . . . it's, like, the only place where people care about how you're doing in school. . . . We get dinner and snacks and we get parties here too. If there was no Center, I would be getting into trouble. People care about me here. Here, everyone's important.

KATIE: I would be miserable [if didn't come to the Center]. I wouldn't have fun. I wouldn't feel like I belonged to anything or anyone . . . I wouldn't be able to communicate with other people; I would be in the fields probably. . . . I feel safe here . . . the people who work here take care of you. It's the only place that helps with homework, and shares games and candy. They also got bread on Mondays. And they got the food bank on Mondays, and we eat dinner here every night at 5 o'clock. They got a special program for us so we could.

ROSIE: If I didn't come [to Center] I would hang out on the corner or in the fields or warehouse. Like, my mother and sister have a serious drug problem, and I would be doing it too if I were home. You see, I come here everyday until ten. . . . Some [girls] come because they want to meet boys. Some of them are cute. Sometimes I go check them out, and Mitchell keeps his eye on them, it's great. . . . If I didn't come I would be smoking up every day and drinking every day. I would be in the back fields . . . but I get with things here. Like, the tutoring program is helping me do good in math. I try to get involved with the most things I can.

CHRISTINA: I feel safe here because there's a whole bunch of people around and there's no place around here where you can get raped or killed because everybody's out and they can't do nothing. . . . I've already gotten raped. It was scary. He threatened to kill me. I was scared . . . I was a kid, under 10 at the time. . . . My mom almost killed him. She was furious. She was biting her tongue. She said that if anybody does this to you again I want to hear it right away. If not, beware. . . . I like everything here. You can play or you can just hang around and you can forget about all the bad things because you're safe. You can have a party for someone's birthday or like for someone who's moving away. I come every day that it's open until 9:30 or 10:00. On Saturdays I come at noon until close.

When asked why they come to the Center, the girls all share similar responses, many of which are based upon an escape from the violence that permeates their lives at home and on the streets. Unlike the uncontrollable outbursts of anger at home, the Center presents a place where there are consistent schedules and rules and where the ideology that "everyone is important" prevails. At the Center, the white Canal Town girls feel they are protected and are given the attention that may be missing from life at home—as Christina says, "people care about me here."

Embedded in many of these poor white girls' descriptions of why the Center is so appealing is that it is a space that is safe from the dangerous male. At home, mothers often are not able to protect their children from abuse at the hands of men, or in some cases, are themselves violent. Christina told me that two years ago she was raped by her mother's former boyfriend, a man who also threatened her young life. For whatever reason, Christina says her mother did not contact authorities and was left "biting her tongue." In a world in which males are menacing, Christina's mother could not promise her daughter that steps would be taken so this would never happen again. Instead, she kept her outrage silent, by telling her daughter if this happened again to let her know and "beware."

In this context, the Center seemingly provides a sense of protection from all males—including boys their own age—from whom the girls also expect tendencies toward aggression. Sally contends she gets to meet "cute boys" at the Center in an environment that gives her more "energy" and "makes me not scared of people." In the same vein, Jamie shares that she "can meet boys [at the Center] and not have to worry about being treated bad." The females, additionally, mention specific public spaces from which they are spared by going to the Center, such as the fields near the river, or an abandoned warehouse down the street, which, along with a few choice street corners, are popular places for drug usage among neighborhood youth. If it were not for the Center, these girls say they can easily see themselves choosing the insides of gutted warehouses, dark fields, or busy street corners—over conditions at home—as places to go after school.

As their narrations indicate, in many ways, the Center also serves as a surrogate functional family. These girls relay they are important when they visit. They say they are encouraged by the staff to work at and to succeed at school, and they mention set hours during which they must do their homework. Perhaps similar to living an idealized home life, white Canal Town girls boast that at the Center, they can help themselves to snacks and refreshments, are served dinners, and celebrate birthdays and other occasions. In keeping with this notion of "family," the females look to the staff, and in particular, Ruby, as someone who has a great impact on their lives.

> HANNAH: Ruby is like a grandmother to me. . . . I could be anywhere and whatever I think I'm like, well, "Ruby wouldn't like that." . . . she haunts me . . . it's like, "Oh, she wouldn't like that!" . . . Because Ruby has opened herself to me, like at Girls' Club. And it makes me feel good, 'cause, you know, I'm only 13 . . . it's like she doesn't see me as a 13-year-old. She just talks to me. She just gives me examples of her life. . . . She's really the main person in my life.

> ANNE: I love my mother . . . but Ruby's just like my best friend. . . . I can't tell my mother anything . . . I don't know why, but I can't sit down and be like, "Well, Mom, guess what I did today?" I don't know why . . . but with Ruby, I just talk to her like about anything . . . before you even mention your problem Ruby knows something is wrong. And it just makes you want to talk about it . . . and then Ruby spends a lot of time with me. She'll take me out places, to the mall. And if I have some kind of event, she'll go. And she'll [Ruby] invite me to her house. She had me over for Thanksgiving because we [at home] usually don't get around to celebrating it.

> LISA: I walk straight from school to here. I talk to Ruby, because I'm always talking to Ruby about different things. I usually do some tutoring or read a book and have a snack. Tonight in Girls' Club we're having a pretend picnic [it is mid-winter]. I can't wait for that . . . it's like

I have somewhere where I can go and relax, play pool, talk to Ruby like always . . . I can meet some of the boys. . . . Girls come here [to the Center] because they love to talk with Ruby. She always helps them, even when it's real bad. If someone wants to beat them up [in school] or something she tells them to walk away or she talks to a teacher. . . . I can talk to Ruby. I talked to her about one of my friends smoking up. I might have to talk to her about it again. The reason why I tell her is because I'm scared for them, and I won't want them to die or anything.

The girls characterize Ruby as fulfilling the role of mother, grandmother, and friend. They say she is both warm and stern at the same time, and they defer to her when they have problems. Through Ruby, it seems, these females seek and are rewarded with some of the adult attention that is missing from their lives. The girls contend they appreciate that Ruby does not treat them like kids, and in dispensing advice, she also shares her life experiences.

Ruby's involvement in the lives of the girls extends far beyond the walls of the community center. For instance, Anne describes how Ruby takes her shopping and has her over for holidays. During my observation year, Ruby had many of the girls over to her house for dinner and even had some sleep over in the summer. Unlike parents, who may be unable or unwilling to take an active role in their daughters' lives, Ruby often seems to step in the ring. For example, Katie is the second oldest child in a family comprised of her pregnant mother, 46, who is an alcoholic, her mother's boyfriend, and seven brothers and sisters. Katie, apparently, has to do a lot of housework and is in complete charge of three younger siblings whom she must watch at the Center. Katie is shy and tells me she is embarrassed her family is so large. I have witnessed Katie distressingly turn to Ruby a number of times, complaining she "has no freedom" and wants "time off" from babysitting her siblings. On at least three occasions in which I accompanied Ruby, we visited Katie's mother, during which time Ruby reminded her that Katie needs some time to herself. Ruby told me she tries to talk to Katie's mother about birth control, and has even taken her to health clinics.

The white Canal Town girls consider Ruby an important person in their lives, even while at school, and they often turn to Ruby, not teachers or parents, when there is a problem. For example, I accompanied Ruby to a conference with a Spanish teacher after Rosie complained she was being unfairly graded. In another instance, Jane, a pregnant girl in the eighth grade, had painful cramps while in school. Jane's teacher sent her to the nurse, and when the cramps started to worsen, she was advised to lay down. Some of the girls did not think the nurse was doing enough, so Anne got on a pay phone and called Ruby at work, who immediately arranged for an ambulance to meet her at the school. Ruby rode with Jane to the hospital, where two hours later, she lost the baby. The white females seem to know Ruby will drop everything and respond to their needs, even if it means she might get in trouble with parents and/or school authorities.

GIRLS' CLUB

Canal Town girls contend they feel a sense of belonging and safety at the Center, the likes of which they do not feel at home or school. Such messages are interpreted by the females in a variety of ways—through the philosophy of the Center, through talking to Ruby and other staff, through unstructured but supervised play with others, through structured recreation, and through participation in organized activities and field trips. One such activity, Girls' Club, is a highly popular club at the Center, drawing forty-seven neighborhood females, which is noteworthy, considering almost every girl attends each week without fail. While this particular club shares a name with the national organization, it is not associated with that larger group. The club, which meets on Wednesday nights from 6:00 until 7:30, is comprised of females, ages 3 to 18. There used to be a separate Girls' Teen Club, which met on Wednesday nights from 7:30 until 9:00, but the two clubs voted to combine membership in order to increase fund-raising efforts and because more grant money could be secured for a larger group. The older girls, Ruby tells me, would always come to the younger club anyway. The females who participate in Girls' Club are mostly white.

It is significant that high school age females from the neighborhood attend Girls' Club, as these older girls do not come to the Center for any other activities. As previously mentioned, beyond middle school, spending time at the Center is seen as "uncool." Ruby is of the belief that ninth through twelfth grade girls continue this weekly event because they did not have much of a childhood, having been forced to confront mature situations at early ages. As part of Girls' Club membership, Ruby has the girls plan their own activities at the end of each month. Interestingly, I observed that the oldest girls voted for activities that would normally be viewed as geared toward little girls—such as baking cupcakes, having indoor picnics, watching Disney videos, making paper dolls, and having tea parties. After attending Girls' Club for one year, I noticed that within Girls' Club, females typically group themselves according to age, and instead of taking on a big sister role, older females tended to participate in activities as if they themselves were young girls.

At the start of Girls' Club, the procedure is that once the night's activity is under way, each female has to have an individual conference with Ruby concerning any problems she might be having. During the many nights that I attended Girls' Club, I was a participant observer during tea parties, cookie baking sessions, Easter bonnet making and decorating, arts-and-crafts workshops, swimming lessons and open swim, and countless birthday and going away parties. During the parties, Ruby, who is an accordian player, provides constant music.

For the last half hour of every Girls' Club, the females sit in a circle while Ruby reminds them to talk to her during the week about any problems. If one of the girls is going through a particularly difficult time, Ruby sometimes talks to the group about how the situation could be improved. For instance, when Jane lost her baby and was recovering at her grandmother's house, Ruby suggested that the girls be extra nice and supportive. The females then decided on some special things they could do, like walk Jane to school. Even those who were as young as 5 years old joined in this conversation, seemingly comprehending all that was said, and a few of the youngest Girls' Club members decided to make Jane a card. Some of the females mention things they specifically learn by talking to Ruby and from Girls' Club—lessons, again, which are juxtaposed with the violence that saturates their lives.

ELIZABETH: From Ruby I've learned not to beat up people. I've learned to stay out of it, because when my mom's boyfriend used to hit my mom, I started screaming at him and stuff, but I've learned to stay out of it. I would scream, "Stop it or I'll call the cops!" I did it once. I called the cops and they came and told him to stop it and they threw him in jail for two days. He knew I called the cops. He knew I had the right. But now he said we can't have a phone anymore. She [her mother] had a fractured arm and a couple of bruises, but she told them [police, doctors] that she got that from falling down the stairs. She just wanted to get him out of jail. . . . We [Ruby and I] talked about trying to stay out of the hitting at home.

ANNE: The Center keeps me out of trouble. I learn more about drugs from speakers we get on Saturday nights, why education is so important, HIV and AIDS, things like that. People from the police department talk about drugs. Some person who has AIDS comes and teaches about it and says it's not really good, because now we know. It's all just from being around here a lot, Ruby, Girls' Club, and swimming lessons; it's all fun. Me and Mindy [her sister] have somewhere to go everyday after school where we get to talk to people and get things to eat and have to do homework. . . . If I didn't come I would be beating up my friends because we wouldn't know you're not supposed to fight. It's, like, people hate each other. They just start fighting and they don't even know what they're doing. Girls hit the boys and the boys hit the girls. Even though the boys ain't supposed to beat up girls, they do and I don't know why.

SALLY: I first started coming [to the Center] through Girls' Club. I joined when I was 5. Like, once my best friend had to move so we had a party for her. We were all crying but it was fun at the same time. I go to Girls' Club because of the activities and it makes you feel better. If you feel all sad and everything, they help and try to make you happy instead of putting you down. Everyone always used to pick on Christina because of the things she used to do [I am told she used to be very sexually active]. Everyone used to call her names and put her down. She always said she wanted to kill herself. Everyone used to call her a whore and everything, and then she finally started calling herself that. So finally in Girls' Club, Ruby asked everyone if they could just be nice to her and tell her she shouldn't think about killing herself.

ERIN: I hear in Girls' Club other girls talk to Ruby about experiences at home that I don't have. . . . I would say they trust Ruby because it's, like, a girl problem. Like, they get beat on by their mom's boyfriend or their dad, and they get abused and stuff, which I really don't so much as them. When I get older I'm not getting married or having kids, so there won't be any to get hit. One of my friends used to get beat on a lot because her father was always drunk. One day she got sick of it and ran away, but she went back after she found out he was sorry for it. If it ever happens to me, I'll tell Ruby during Girls' Club.

The females reveal that on an individual basis during Girls' Club, they talk to Ruby about problems in their lives, much of which includes abuse. Although Erin indicates that in the all-girl space of Girls' Club, the girls know about the violence in each other's lives, it is ultimately coped with in private talk with Ruby and/or in isolation. Just as these girls mentioned that adult women in their lives at times reach out to other females after being abused, there continues to be an absence of any sense of male accountability, as Erin describes domestic violence as a "girl problem." It appears, instead, at very young ages, these girls learn from other females that it is their duty to persevere. This outlook is also not disrupted at the Center.

One afternoon when I was in the kitchen of the Center talking to Ruby, Elizabeth came in to say hello, and then suddenly burst into tears. When she was able to calm down, she told us her mother's boyfriend got angry with her for waking him up that morning, so he grabbed the coffee pot and threw boiling water at her, scalding her arm. I watched Ruby hug Elizabeth, carefully bandage her arm, make her some hot chocolate, and tell her that she was smart and beautiful and that she would amount to something. Although nowhere in Ruby's kind words was there any suggestion that it is wrong for men to act out in violence, she is not a counselor, and it is not her job to act as one. What the data reveal, however, is that forums such as Girls' Club *do* exist in which these females, like other girls, could learn to collectively view domestic violence as an epidemic assault against women, and where they could learn to develop a critique of men and family. In such a space, they *could* potentially move beyond the notion that violence is simply a part of life, and if they find fortitude within themselves, they will survive. For now, these white females view the space of the Center, and in particular Girls' Club, as an escape from violent homes and "minorities" who are thought to be invading their neighborhood and school. In the Center, these females suggest, they are not afraid to be little girls.

BOYS

When asked what the Center means to them, the poor white Canal Town boys characterize it as a place to go where they feel a sense of importance. While some of these males say they avail themselves of swimming lessons and open swim and Boys' Club, all of them position, in particular, the gym as a place of intense meaning and in opposition to their dissatisfaction with life on the streets and in school. In those places, struggles around the construction of white male identity have been seen to coalesce around racial border patrolling. In the view of these boys, authorities—such as the principal, teachers, and officials at City Hall—are encouraging "minorities" to take over.

As seen previously, these boys are angry that Felicia can only procure funding for the Center if Puerto Rican youth are in attendance, a sentiment they likely picked up from Mitchell and perhaps others in their lives. This act of blaming "minorities" for monopolizing resources, for instance, may also be learned from some of their white teachers at school. On the floor of the gym, these white boys bestow upon themselves a sense of superiority. By staking out an all-white and all-male space in the gym, these boys animate a sense of white manhood that is both virulent and highly prized, a script they feel have been denied them in other places.

JAMES: The Center is like my favorite place in the world, like the gym here. I love the pool; it's so cool to swim in the winter and, like, Boys' Club, but the gym is the best. I play on all the sports teams all year long—basketball, baseball, hockey, football. It's like they [staff at Center] give us [white Canal Town boys] the right to practice and play in the gym whenever we want. Even if Mitchell ain't in, we can, like, get the key to storage, take out the equipment, and start a pick-up game whenever we want. Mitchell lets us do whatever we want. We can be by ourselves practicing, not like school, where we got to play on teams with girls and those Puerto Rican guys. . . . It's, like, at school, the gym teacher purposefully breaks up any of us guys [Canal Town boys] on different teams. If we were together at school on any team, I don't care what sport, we'd wipe of the floor with everyone else. We'd turn them all into girls.

ANDREW: The gym here [at the Center] is my best thing in the world. . . . I go to Friday night open swim, and I'm on all the teams— football, baseball, hockey, you name it, basketball. That's really what I do in life. I come every day at like 3:30 and stay until 10:00. I just play sports with the guys. It's what we do, like our own world. Mitchell spent time with me teaching me how to get better at, like, hockey. Now I'm teaching my little brother. I know how to coach now. Sometimes Mitchell has me coach for the younger guys. Another thing we do here is play pool, eight ball and stuff. Me and my friends play, like every night. . . . It's just us here; we shut the door so no whiney girls can get in. Like at school, you got to play floor hockey with a bunch of Puerto Ricans and girls that suck at it. . . . Everyone in gym at school is just a girl as far as I'm concerned.

PETER: It's great just being in the sports here [at the Center]. In the gym, Mitchell taught me the tricks of the trade in hockey and basketball. . . . I come every day, right after school, and I leave about 9:30, and we practice all day Saturday. . . . We aren't allowed to play serious, with just ourselves in school, and there we can't pick our own teams. We're, like, forced to have people who suck on our teams there, girls and Spanish fags. Here [the Center] we do some coaching for the younger guys. Here we're in control. . . . Mitchell and them [other employees] want us to practice.

JOHN: The things I like here are swim, they have that on Friday nights, Boys' Club, and sports most of all. It's, like, Mitchell allows us [Canal Town boys] to be in control of the gym. . . . At school, we got to play [during gym class] with minority assholes; they play like a bunch of girls. Here at the Center, if, like, anyone walks through the gym to interrupt us when we're practicing, Mitchell told us we can tell them to get the fuck out. They [community center staff] really like us to do our thing, you know, practice.

The narrations of the Canal Town boys reveal that the gym floor at the Center becomes a space for the production of a concentrated form of maleness *and* whiteness. Current research on working class white boys suggests that masculinity develops "oppositionally" to white women, gay men, and women and men from culturally oppressed

groups (Willis, 1977; Weis, 1990; Connell, 1993). Like poor and working class white older males (Weis, 1990; Fine et al., 1997), these boys are
reacting to the effects of feminism, affirmative action, and global
restructuring by positioning "others" as "robbing" them of their relative
privilege. Such notions are arguably enacted without interruption on the
gym floor of the Center.

As argued by Addelston & Stirratt (1996), all-male spaces such as
college fraternities (Sanday, 1990), high school and college sports
teams (Messner & Sabo, 1990, 1994), and/or an exclusively male college campus have been described as a significant location for the
development of negative attitudes toward women and gay men.
Research on the production of sexism and heterosexism in such sites
reveals the raw material from which gender "rules" are constructed
(Connell, 1987). According to these rules, anything feminine is seen
to hinder the production of manhood. Gay men, therefore, stereo-
typed as feminine, are considered a serious threat to "hardcore" manhood (Messner & Sabo, 1990, 1994; Connell, 1993; Klein, 1993;
Polk, 1994). The intersection of race in the construction of manhood,
however, is largely ignored in the literature.

The Canal Town boys seemingly set up the gym at the Center as in
opposition to the diverse space of the athletic court at school. During
any given school gym period for the advanced grades, classes are typically comprised of a mix of white Canal Town girls and boys, Puerto
Rican girls and boys, and African American girls and boys. James complains the school gym teacher purposefully separates him and his friends
when dividing students into teams. In his view, this is an attempt by the
school to pull apart the tightly bound core of virulent white manhood
among the white male group, lest they "wipe up the floor" with everyone else. Due to the presence of "others" on the school gym floor, the
Canal Town boys characterize that space as a diluted place in which to
enact a sense of manhood.

The data indicate the poor white Canal Town boys co-produce their
own identities by emasculating males of Puerto Rican descent, thereby
building up their own sense of white maleness. In trying to establish
their identity as superior, these white boys assert that the other males on
the school gym floor—the Puerto Rican boys—play like girls. This construction is at least partially in response to the white boys' feelings that
"minorities" are taking over their neighborhood and school, and are
seemingly eroding their sense of felt privilege. One could also speculate
about the extent to which the white boys may be threatened by the
stereotype of the sexual prowess of Puerto Rican males. As many of the
white Canal Town boys call the Puerto Rican males "girls," and as one
student makes reference to "Spanish fags," these white males attempt to

subordinate the Puerto Rican boys by scripting them as effeminate, and thus, as the literature suggests, link misogyny with homophobia.

As the Canal Town boys interpret the streets and school as denying them the space to impose their maleness and whiteness as a group, their elaborations of white masculinity at the gym at the Center arguably becomes a crucial site in the formation of identity. The boys explain they spend a lot of time at the Center gym, and feel their time on the gym floor is important to the community center staff. They boast they are given the "right" to practice and help themselves to equipment whenever they please. Many, additionally, take on the role of "expert," as they are also involved in coaching the sports teams of younger white boys. Andrew talks about time spent in the gym at the Center with his white male friends as "our own little world."

In an earlier chapter, when asked about problems with relationships with girls their own age, in many cases, the boys revealed their potential as present and future perpetrators of violence against females. Such attitudes became particularly apparent in relation to the idea of girls infiltrating sports. Sam was very angry over the fact that the first female goalie was let into the National Hockey League, and Randy told how he has hit girls on the playing field at school a number of times. Peter also contended that females should just stay out of men's sports. As already mentioned, two years before my observational year, I learned that Mitchell allowed Erin to play temporarily on the Canal Town boys' baseball team, as one of the boys was injured. I am told Erin only lasted for two games, and when asked about the experience today, she says she was ridiculed to such a extent she decided to quit. Many of the Canal Town boys say they are still angry at Erin for breaking into their carefully guarded white male space. Today Mitchell says he regrets allowing Erin to play as "she wasn't up for it."

In constructing a sense of self, the Center does not obstruct the practice among these white boys of positioning girls as contaminating their space. While watching the boys practice floor hockey from the gymnasium door at the Center, I observed in a number of instances that if white or Puerto Rican girls walked through the gym, they were often verbally attacked using violent images. On one occasion, Tammy, Katie, and three of her little sisters were cutting through the gym, on the way from the pool hall to the senior side. While walking along the wall, out of the way of the game, Jack yelled, "Get out before you get your fucking period all over the floor! If you don't run, we'll bash your heads in!" In the situation with Erin in which gender codes were temporarily broken, even though Mitchell "allowed" her to play on the boys' baseball team, he tells me he will never permit this again because "girls are just not dependable enough to stick it out on a boys' team."

The white Canal Town boys continue to direct considerable anger toward Erin. For instance, Erin is the only girl I observed never to cut through the gym, preferring instead to go outside and walk around the back of the building to the front door, even in the winter night. When I queried her about this habit, she said that since the baseball experience, she is "afraid to be alone with the boys." Insofar as it does not interrupt such practices, the Center, then, encourages these violent attitudes toward white females, those from culturally oppressed groups, and gay males.

While most of the Canal Town boys say they first got involved in the Center by coming with older brothers or friends, some explain that their friends encouraged them to turn to the Center to be "saved." Today, these boys continue to enjoy a sense of belonging. Like the white girls, these young males look to Mitchell and Ruby as people who are extremely important in their lives, and who have often fulfilled the role of caretaker. From Mitchell, Ruby, and programs at the Center, these boys say they learn to reject the drug abuse they witness at home.

SAM: I come as long as it's open because I don't want to get involved with the drugs at home. . . . Like, my mom and the guy friends she has over do heroin and pot. I learned here that you can get AIDS from drugs and sex. I try to stay away. I'm here all day Saturday too. The baseball, basketball, hockey, and football here is my life. . . . I used to be addicted to pot. I finally went to Mitchell and he listened to me and had me talk to Ruby too. I asked her what to do. I told her I couldn't stop. She told me that I could stop it if it was in my heart. So I stopped. It was hard. . . . Every time someone offered me pot I got anxious and walked away. They [other kids] started calling me names . . . but Mitchell and Ruby were watching for me. . . . Like I said, the Center, the sports here is my life.

CHRIS: The Center, like, saved me. Like, through the guys [white Canal Town boys] playing sports, they encouraged me to turn my life around . . . I just wanted to straighten my life out. . . . I once robbed a car and burned it in the back fields. Some older kids, in high school, dared me to do it. I got caught by the cops. . . . Once at school, in the parking lot, I got in a fight with this kid. He started hitting me with a stick so I cut him with a knife . . . I found the knife about a week before in the old warehouse and kept it in my pocket. I barely cut him but it was on school grounds. . . . His parents were going to press charges but they didn't because some of my friends told the cops they saw him come up to me from behind. . . . The guys told me to talk to Mitchell. I told Mitchell I was sick of killing my brain cells with smoking, drinking, lots of pot . . . my mom does drugs at home and that gets me into it. . . . He [Mitchell] started me in sports, first with the basketball team.

I started to come to practice every day after school and all day Saturday. I'm hardly ever at home now. Now I'm on all the teams. I feel better now. When I used to run, I would get halfway around the gym and my stomach started hurting. Now when I run it don't bother me.

ROBBIE: My dad does a lot of drugs. People even come over to our house to get it from him. . . . Ruby tells me it's not good to do drugs because you end up hurting yourself and wasting your life. . . . Ruby, Mitchell, and me thought it was good for me to come here [the Center] as much as I can, like from right after school 'til late. . . . I love it here. I love our gym. I love swimming . . .

The Canal Town boys view Mitchell and Ruby as responsible adults whom they can turn to when things get bad. When one of the boys has a problem, they typically first talk to Mitchell, who in some instances then brings the situation to Ruby's attention. Sam, Chris, and Robbie critique adults at home for living in an unhealthy environment due to drug activity. Unlike Girls' Club, where each female has to formally report to Ruby, Ruby tells me the boys meet with her when they need to on an informal basis.

Mitchell's and Ruby's involvement in the white boys' lives, in some cases, is quite extensive. Often this level of commitment to neighborhood youth results in opposition from parents, and indeed, many of the boys have learned from the Center or from friends who have introduced them to the Center that the drug usage in their homes is bad. One day at the Center, I found that Peter was being held in a juvenile detention center because he was caught selling marijuana and heroin. Mitchell and Ruby were frantic because they believed Peter's mother was forcing her son to push for her. When they tried to convince child authorities of this, Peter denied his mother's involvement in his decision to sell drugs, and was placed in a detention home for three months. Mitchell and Ruby later angrily concluded they could understand why a child would want to cover for a parent, but they could not comprehend how a parent could exploit a child. On another occasion, one afternoon Mitchell brought Andrew over to Ruby for a talk. Andrew, who looked very frightened, explained while he was getting ready for school that morning, he stepped on a used heroin needle that was on the kitchen floor. Since the needle punctured his skin and drew blood, Andrew was convinced he now had AIDS. Ruby had a long talk with Andrew, telling him she was sure he was safe, and the way his mother was living was wrong, but as long as he took precautions in the future, he would remain healthy. These words seemed to calm Andrew down. Some of the Canal Town boys talk about other reassuring things they hear and learn at the Center.

SAM: Like at the Center, I learn how to be a really good athlete. . . . I also learn I can talk to Mitchell and Ruby about my problems. I'm learning you can change your life . . . I learn this by talking to Ruby. . . . I learn to look out for my friends . . . if one of the guys is in trouble, I'd help right away. . . . I learn from, like, Mitchell and Ruby to be, like, proud of who I am, proud of the neighborhood.

RANDY: An important thing I learned from here [the Center] is that you got to look out for your own sometimes. That's what they [employees] do here. They look after us kids and the neighborhood. They stick up for us.

ANDREW: I'm practicing for my future here [Center gymnasium], to be a professional athlete. I learn about being on a team here [Center], and how important it is to look out for each other. . . . Ruby tells me not everything in life is fair, but if you stay out of trouble and work to keep trouble away, you're a better person for it. If one of the guys [white friends] was in trouble, I'd try to help. If you don't stick together as a group, others are going to take advantage . . . by others, I mean like minorities taking over the neighborhood, taking over the school; next thing you'll know, they'll try and take over the Center. I'll tell you, it's going to be a cold day in Hell when that happens. The guys and I would never let it happen.

JACK: It's, like, we learn here to stay away from trouble—drugs, alcohol, AIDS. We learn about protecting ourselves, our neighborhood, our Center from trouble. There are a lot of criminals coming into the neighborhood, some of them go to our school . . . I mean, like, minorities. They cause trouble and then get special treatment. Well, I know one place were they ain't going to get royal treatment, here [the Center]. Me and my friends think the white people who try hard and try to do what's right are the ones who should get the goodest treatment. I don't care what City Hall and damn politicians say, or them [administrators; teachers] at the school.

The poor white Canal Town boys maintain that at the Center, they learn they can talk about their problems with community center staff, in the absence of what they think are uncaring parents or teachers. Through talking to Mitchell and Ruby, and listening to Saturday guest speakers, the boys see the Center as a place that offers an alternative lifestyle to the drug usage that may be going on at home. As these narrations indicate, boys who are regular visitors to the Center have been known to try to spare their friends from drug addiction by bringing them to the Center and having Mitchell and Ruby take over.

At the same time, however, the Center does not deter the production of a virulent form of racism, sexism, and homophobia. As described in gym class at school, the white boys conflate racism, misogyny, and homophobia in an attempt to construct a sense of self as superior (Messner & Sabo, 1990; Connell, 1993; Klein, 1993; Polk, 1994). And as depicted in an earlier chapter, these white boys have the potential to direct extreme violence toward white females and those from culturally oppressed groups. Beyond the anti-drug programming, it seems the Center's way of getting the Canal Town young males to realize a life different from the one at home is to let them have free rein in the gym. In an attempt to make these boys feel valued and worthwhile, the Center encourages them to develop into serious athletes in this all-male and all-white space, and therefore, does not disrupt their elaborations of white male supremacy. With his own anger toward white females and the cultural "other," Mitchell also arguably promotes these tendencies within the boys.

Just as they have learned to critique drug usage, forums *do* exist at the Center in which the Canal Town boys *could* dismantle racism, sexism, and homophobia. For now, the sum of the experiences of the young males at the Center may ultimately add up to a sense of "looking out" for each other. As Andrew explains, he has learned it is crucial to stick together as a group, otherwise "others" will "take advantage." Andrew goes on to clarify that he is referring to those of Puerto Rican and African descent he feels are "taking over" the neighborhood and the school. For these white boys, the Center is their final holdout.

The staff's efforts to keep area white youth from experimenting with drugs and involved in homework may stem from their perception that "minorities" are "taking over." Since, in the view of some of the Center employees, those from culturally oppressed groups are given all the advantages and resources by school administrators and policymakers, the fear may be that the white youth will end up like many white adults—involved in unlawful activity, thus *giving* "minorities" the opportunity to step in and take over. Actions are taken by Felicia, Ruby, and Mitchell, therefore, to make sure the space of the Center is home-like, so that white local youth are given the chance to develop seemingly healthy lifestyles. In order to afford the "extra" things needed to sustain this agenda at the Center, employees extend themselves outside into the community, with the goal of making connections to potential funding sources. In cases in which those at the Center want to "lobby" for change, alliances are formed with similarly thinking neighborhood institutions and publics, and white youth are encouraged to help.

I argue that those interested in social change must think about life outside the school in trying to make sense of adolescent meaning-making processes. Feeling pushed out of their homes, streets, and the school, the poor white Canal Town youth turn to the Center for a sense of relief and belonging. Inside this space, adults involve youth in political projects geared toward changing things for what they feel is the good of the community. I contend, however, that these goals are organized toward sustaining the ideology of white supremacy. Through the deliberate action of white adults, Canal Town youth are learning to rely upon community resources and to make connections with other agencies and institutions in order to strengthen a racist agenda. The community center, therefore, can be seen as a powerful place in the transmission of white supremacy.

CHAPTER 7

Youth and the Future

It is eight o'clock in the evening on a warm June night, and the senior side of the Center is packed with people; Felicia is about to call a meeting to order. Just two weeks ago, Felicia learned at a City Council session that the State Thruway Department was seriously considering Canal Town as the location for a truck weighing station and parking lot. As Felicia explains, this plan is proposed for the site on which the Center stands, and, as she says, "would effectively dissolve our Irish community." Felicia responded to this news by putting her network into motion—calling leaders of the North Side and Riley Road community centers, representatives from area industry, local politicians, and city media to this meeting. The goal of the gathering, relays Felicia, is to make "a formal and unified statement to protest this action." Felicia also had the white Canal Town youth distribute leaflets to all the homes in the area informing citizens of the event. Although there are hardly any parents in attendance, the room is brimming with the voices of invited guests, Canal Town senior citizens, and local youth. Having done their homework, eaten dinner, and practiced in the gym, the youth have come to offer support to save their neighborhood.

In this ethnographic study, I explored the construction of gendered identities among a group of poor white middle school youth in a bilingual school and community center, both located in Canal Town. As stated earlier, I understand identity as various and changing conceptions of self, where meaning is forged along points of individual and collective experience, social institutions, and economic structures which mediate the production of notions of race, ethnicity, class, and gender (Hicks, 1981; Crenshaw, 1989; McCarthy, 1990). I also contend that in order to gain a fuller understanding of processes of meaning making, analyses must be textualized within an examination of a group's cultural history.

The history of Canal Town reveals much about the contemporary economic, political, and social life of the neighborhood. Hired to dig the Midwestern Canal, many Irish laborers worked across the state and ended up in Canal Town, as it was the last stop on the waterway. Once in the area, workers and their families found jobs that revolved around the canal. In Canal Town, Irish laborers were resentful of the Protestant business elite who controlled the economy. Using historically inscribed racism to their advantage, capital used Black labor to break strikes and compete for low wages, with the goal of keeping class consciousness from forming. Encouraged by the efforts of capital, for many generations, during the construction of an Irish working class identity, anger continued to be deflected off capital, and onto those from culturally oppressed groups (Roediger, 1994).

Racism toward "others," however, existed long before industrialization, and has much deeper historical underpinnings (Ani, 1994). Before coming to the United States, the Irish were participating in a white supremacist system. Leaving their poverty-stricken homeland, Irish immigrants came to the urban centers in the North, where they found that social status was, to a large extent, based upon color—a concept, some argue, they did not have to confront as much back in Ireland due to the isolated nature of rural life (Roediger, 1994; Ignatiev, 1995). Discriminated against, many could find only low-paying, hard labor jobs—working in coal mines, digging canals, and, later, building railroads, Irish workers were positioned just one step up from Black laborers. Fueled by capital's manipulations of racism, in defining a sense of self as superior, Irish workers actively participated in rendering those of African descent in a racialized subgroup (Roediger, 1994). In some cases, the children of Irish immigrants were able to fare better than those from the east and south of Europe due to their ability to speak English (Takaki, 1993). Because of their language skills, the Irish may have emigrated to the United States with a sense of entitlement to good jobs that was further developed while living alongside communities of people from other cultural/linguistic backgrounds.

Takaki (1993) recounts how many Irish immigrants retained a sense of Irish identity and solidarity in the United States by passing down stories of Anglo oppression. In terms of Canal Town, Felicia, Ruby, Mitchell, and the elderly residents retain a sense of Irish pride in their ancestors' contributions to digging the canal and "opening up the city." Although in narrating a sense of group importance, references are made to the hard work of Irish immigrants, missing is mention of their ancestors' struggles in the context of British domination. It seems that among Irish Americans in Canal Town today, anger directed toward the business class has been diffused and displaced upon "others" to such an extent that this critique has simply faded away. In Canal Town, it appears that all that is left of Irish solidarity is the St. Patrick's Day celebration, a few shamrocks pasted year-round on the Center walls, and anger directed toward those from culturally oppressed groups who are believed to be "infiltrating" the tight-knit community.

Today, particularly among the white Canal Town boys, a sense of racism emerges that is narrated in a discourse of lost entitlement. As mentioned, while their ancestors were driven from Ireland by the British elite, due to their ability to speak English, these immigrants likely came to the United States "expecting more." In parallel ways, the poor white Canal Town boys inherit anger for their economic dislocations, but displace it on a few low-level governance officials, and most specifically, "minorities." As their articulations indicate, for the most part, the poor white youth have not learned to draw upon family and community cultural history in trying to make sense of their place in the world. Instead, through generations, Irish working solidarity in the face of British oppression has come to be deeply buried underneath a thick blanket of whiteness. In efforts to maintain a sense of importance in a climate of poverty, these poor white girls and boys have been socialized to engage in virulent displacements.

The present-day racism and domestic violence experienced within this community must be examined in the context of cultural amnesia. As Irish American male workers historically clashed with Black laborers on the docks of Canal Town, racism toward those from culturally oppressed groups has been further encouraged among generations of white families. With the onset of deindustrialization, Black workers, and to an extent, white females, were continuously positioned by white male laborers as responsible for the erosion of opportunities to bring home a family wage. Feeling socially and economically devalued, white working class males continued to exert dominance in the home (Smith, 1987). Although domestic violence existed long before the days of industry, white working class gender relations—which dictated that white women were subordinate to white men—encouraged the silencing and normalizing of this behavior. Today, devoid of any sense of critical cultural history, the poor white Canal Town girls learn to "work around" violence and take part in a "culture of concealment." Hideously, these girls have come to position males from culturally oppressed groups as their victimizers and white males as their protectors, even though at home many are being beaten by white males.

In constructing a sense of self inscribed with value through competing symbolic and material lived social practices, these poor white youth are discursively learning from their families, the school, and the community center that racism, domestic violence, and poverty are normal behaviors and/or conditions. Identities, as stated, are multifaceted and changing notions of self, produced along points of individual and collective experience, social institutions, and economic structures. For the poor white Canal Town youth, at different points in time, various facets of identity are likely more salient than others. When confronted with abuse, for example, the poor white Canal Town girls likely experience their gendered selves the most. While speaking disparagingly about youth from culturally oppressed groups, they perhaps primarily assert notions of race. When they participate in Girls' Club, the poor white girls seemingly elaborate upon a sense of childhood as most prominent. With the absence of any critical sense of cultural history, however, all these points of meaning are built upon major displacements, to such an extent, that inhumane actions are seen as commonplace. As the history of Irish Americans in the United States demonstrates, in co-constructing identity relationally, through the generations, the focus on those who are positioned as "other" has shifted. Instead of acknowledging their historically adversarial relationship with an Anglo or business elite which has sold them out, over time, this part of the Irish experience in Canal Town has become throughly anesthetized. Although identities shift and change in Canal Town, today they mutate against a backdrop in which whiteness is reified.

Growing up in an environment of poverty, violence, and felt lost entitlement, the poor white youth of Canal Town narrate that the Center is a place of importance in their lives. As I argue in this research, in trying to understand how poor urban youth construct identities, it is crucial to peer inside those spaces adolescents designate as important. Fine and Weis (1998) maintain that poor and working class adults from various cultural backgrounds are "homesteading," or creatively carving out spaces in daily life in which to safely engage in collective political critique with the objective of constructing hopeful visions for the future. As described by the poor white youth of Canal Town, the local community center is also "home-like," as it offers support, guidance, safety, and meaning.

As a space organized by adults for youth, the Canal Town community center is not simply a place for children to go to feel good. Seemingly paralleling the type of "free space" as described by Evans and Boyte (1992), the Center can be said to resemble the space between private lives and institutional structures, inside which citizens *do* learn to critically participate in what they think to be meaningful change. As voices from various areas of social life from outside are called upon and pulled inside, the space allows for disparate objectives to be hammered out through debate. The Center is a site of intense political work, in which, alongside adults, youth learn to collectively critique their social realities and mobilize toward change.

Although in some ways fitting the definition of a "free space" (Evans & Boyte, 1992), it must be acknowledged that in locations such as the Center, individuals are working toward collective goals guided by an ideology of white supremacy. As seen at the Center, although relationships are formed with larger and diverse patterns of decision making—for example, with politicians, businesspeople, and representatives from other community centers—there is a conscious effort on behalf of staff members to include only those voices and sources that can be shaped to fit their goals. After all, as a product of history, the "colonial discourse" of white supremacy does not just "exist," but is continuously labored upon and passed down through generations; places such as the Canal Town community center act as a base upon which the scaffolding of such thinking is maintained.

Those interested in social transformation must push outside school walls in trying to make sense of how youth construct identities. By entering into those spaces in which children go to gain composure and strength, a more substantial understanding of how youth struggle to make meaning is found. Compared to the formal and controlled space of a school, in the informal and predominantly white site of the community center, I learned of an emerging sense of racism within the identities of the poor white girls. In this location, I also found both the white girls and boys were confronted with domestic violence on a daily basis. If I had gathered data in only the school, similar to other ethnographies that explore the formation of identity among white youth, I likely would not have picked up on such issues (Willis, 1977; Valli, 1988; Weis, 1990). I also, additionally, would not have realized the school was doing nothing to interrupt potential patterns of racist, sexist, and homophobic violence. As the poor white Canal Town girls ascribe to racist mythology in positioning males of African descent and those who are Puerto Rican that "seem" Black as their violators, they further participate in their own victimization. As long as educators continue to leave such attitudes unacknowledged, these forms of oppression will continue to be silenced, and also will continue to grow in strength. As long as adults position youth as "too young" or not "mature" enough to handle open discussion, we are selectively forcing them out into the world to experience and/or participate in violent forms of denigration, and teaching them to think this is "normal."

Researchers, teachers, and community leaders must somehow work together to see the importance of opening up ongoing, critical dialogue pertaining to racism and domestic violence across sites. In the school and the Center, youth must critically research their cultural history, and learn to view their realities as socially and historically constructed. By seeing themselves as part of an Irish American legacy, the "monolith" of whiteness can be seen as made up of a series of cultures, and then *can* be decentered. Instead of blaming low-level government and "minorities" for their troubles, all children must collaboratively learn to analyze their cultural-historical place within the shifting economy. Throughout the data, there is a profound sense among the poor white youth that poverty is also somehow "normal." By seeing themselves as a part of cultural history, white area youth can begin to see this as a result of extreme displacements. Youth must be encouraged to analyze *why*—in terms of their cultural history—they do not wake up each morning, look out the window, and see a whole community going to work.

As the history of Canal Town suggests, racism existed even during times of relative prosperity, and has much more invasive historical roots (Ani, 1994). This must be emphasized in educative sites, as well as the fact that we all act out of frameworks that have been historically constructed to benefit an Anglo-European elite, a fact that has been leveled off to such an extent among poor, working class, and middle-class individuals of the dominant culture, that there is often little realization that their needs are not being served. White youth must also begin to take responsibility for harmfully affecting other people. By learning to view those who truly hold economic control over their lives and make them accountable, people could potentially mobilize towards more structural change. This will only happen if poor and working class white individuals act in *solidarity* with those from culturally dominated groups.

At school and the Center, youth can be taught to critically analyze the ideology of the family wage in a collective fashion. In order not to repeat the same "cycles of abuse" as their mothers, together as a group, these youth can begin to hold white males accountable for their abusive behavior. Youth must be led to see the historical interconnections among race, ethnicity, class, and gender in the formation of group identities. It has been argued, for example, that forms of violence against females is a powerful tool of racism that has historically served to strengthen the notion of white supremacist patriarchal control. Davis (1981) asserts that sexism and domestic violence can be seen as fundamentally linked to racism, as during institutionalized enslavement, racism encouraged sexism in that white men believed they "owned" the bodies of African American women, men, and children. Davis reports that slave-owners assumed the license to rape Black women, and that today, white men can still believe that their whiteness and maleness accords them the privilege to dominate *all* females. By talking as a group about intersections of race and class in relation to abuse, the white youth of Canal Town can be encouraged to see their vantage points as contextualized within socially and historically constructed systems of domination and oppression, and thus changeable.

As this research shows, people are struggling to respond to structures which they believe shut them out. The Canal Town community center and countless other "safe" spaces in poor and working class urban neighborhoods are a testament to this point. Although the Center in Canal Town ultimately works to reify whiteness, male dominance, and heterosexuality, forums such as Girls' Club and Boys' Club do exist in which life *could* be reimagined in counter-hegemonic ways. While such critical responses to social reality can take place in schools, the space of the Center—unbounded by state, local administrative, and parental surveillance—can attend to dismantling the forces of oppression in bold and much more forthright ways. By networking with others whose perspectives are truly diverse, socially transformative voices could multiply in strength.

As seen at the Center, nutritional, educational, and other support services are geared toward helping people across the life span. It is crucial, however, not to glorify such places, as in selectively doling out services, they do not substitute for the days of the past in which families could choose in a more private manner how they spend assistance. As I demonstrate in this analysis, as neighborhood organizations such as the Canal Town Center move toward the role of comprehensive service provider, only select people may feel welcome to avail themselves of programs. In the case of Canal Town, those from culturally oppressed groups are systematically excluded.

It must be emphasized that just below the radar screen, many community organizations likely do provide space and encouragement for positive identity work. Educators have much to learn from these sites. Those interested in social change, however, must also enter spaces such as the Canal Town Center in order to get a better sense of the development of oppressive community ideology, and how such thinking is distributed among youth. As seen in this study, there are many ways in which the poor white Canal Town youth are experiencing the world that were not obvious inside the school. My whiteness arguably helped me gain acceptance inside the carefully guarded space of the Canal Town Center. Once inside, I began to learn what happens among some people, when others are not looking. By spending time in such locations, educators can gain the knowledge needed to contribute meaningfully to the shaping of public policy that is grounded in the promotion of anti-racism and anti-violence. For the sake of impoverished urban youth, educators must take part in welfare debates *and* think of ways to fill these spaces with meaningful dialogue.

NOTES

CHAPTER 1. INTRODUCTION

1. "Canal Town" is the name I give to the historically white and industrial section of the northern city in which this study takes place.

2. Although MacLeod (1987) looks at the lives of low-income African American and white teenage males in a housing project, the research considers the experiences of only males, and was conducted during the early 1980s, during a time when jobs in industry were arguably still available.

3. These narrations are included in Chapter 2.

4. A discussion of the public assistance recipient status/employment history concerning the families of the poor white youth in this study is presented in Chapter 2.

5. In 1832, 4.5 miles on the shores of Lake _____ were incorporated as the City of _____. What I call "Canal Town" exists today, and remains the oldest district within the city. Having been the original home of the Mohawk, in 1790, European colonials killed and then drove those remaining to settle along the banks of the _____ Creek. With the end of the American Revolution, Royal Charter Grants assigned the entirety of the area to the State of Massachusetts. Robert Morris, a financier of the American Revolution, purchased the property rights from that state, and in 1793 conveyed them to the American trustees of a coterie of Dutch capitalists, the Windsor Land Company. Various indigenous titles were extinguished at this time. Before the arrival of the Irish, the small population of Europeans consisted of Anglo-European Yankees who had migrated from New England and eastern New York State and Pennsylvania. Surrounded by a rapidly growing white population, the Mohawk reportedly lived in constant fear and destitution (Ketchum, 1865; Hotchkin, 1848; Larned, 1911).

6. Historians contend that Irish laborers were hired to dig the Midwestern Canal because they were a ready and cheap labor source, and, unlike other immigrant populations, they were able to speak English (Severance, 1908; Brown & Watson, 1981).

7. Today in Canal Town, the original offices of the longshoremen's union, which were established during this era, still exist.

8. These early immigrants paved the way for later waves of members of these same ethnic groups to come to this city (Walter, 1958).

9. The area was the site of several stops on the Underground Railroad (Hosmer, 1880; Poole, 1905).

10. Historians argue that Canal Town and the larger city was the place where minstrelsy became known as a highly respectable form of entertainment.

Ned Christy came from Philadelphia to Canal Town in 1839, and in the cabaret halls within the district, performed his minstrel show. Word soon leaked out to the more gentrified sections of the city, and the area elite were eager to see the production. Christy's act was then booked outside Canal Town, in the "proper" Milwaukee Street Theater, where it was viewed with enthusiasm by an upper business class clientele. This run, it is said, helped to legitimize minstrelsy, and cleared the way for Christy's institutionalization on Broadway and success in London. Tom Rice, and his "Jim Crow"character, also played to packed white audiences in the city during the 1940s and 1950s (Hosmer, 1880; Shea, 1900; Poole, 1905).

11. The reform-minded Anglo community in the city supported the transportation of all Africans back to Africa. Some of the area's most prominent people at the time were vocal members and directors of the American Colonization Society. Due to historically inscribed racism and competition for wages, German and Irish immigrant communities supported this plan to rid the country of an African population (American Colonization Society, 1835, 1937; Severance, 1907).

12. The white community rationalized their disassociation from people of African descent by supporting stereotypes of intellectual inferiority, promiscuity, and laziness. For instance, the white superintendent of education in 1843 lectured about the slower mental capacity of Black children (City Records, 1843).

13. Immigration to the area has been relatively recent among those from some countries. National immigration policy barred permanent residents from China from 1880 until 1940, while those from Japan were denied access with exclusionary agreements and laws until the 1950s. Since the 1950s, immigrants from China, Japan, India, Korea, Yemen, and Pakistan have come to the city. Puerto Rican immigration to the area began mainly in the 1950s (Brown & Watson, 1981).

CHAPTER 2. ENTERING THE WORLD OF CANAL TOWN

1. From this point forward, I refer to the Canal Town community center as "the Center," as this is the language used by attending youth.

2. I later learned there were a few exceptions: older boys who used the weight room at night and high school females who would come to Wednesday night Girls' Club. Also, teenagers would occasionally show up for the dinner program and food bank.

3. I was also told by a number of poor white Canal Town girls and boys that a common practice among families is to look for a "fast apartment." This means, I am told, that families are always looking for less expensive apartments in the neighborhood in the case that rent can no longer be paid or when property forecloses. In the year in which I collected data, many of the youth moved to different apartments around Canal Town. Elizabeth, for instance, moved six times during the year.

4. The youth told me their parents' ages.

CHAPTER 3. CANAL TOWN GIRLS

1. The white Canal Town girls do not express the amount of contempt for African American females that they do for African American males. This is not to suggest these white girls are not racist toward African American females. In the confines of this study, however, the focus is on expressed anger about males of African American descent, and is linked, in part, to the stereotype of the sexual perpetrator.

2. My work has been greatly influenced by the work of Lois Weis and Michelle Fine and their recent findings from their large-scale Spencer Foundation project designed to capture narrations of poor and working class white, Latina/Latino, and African American young adults as to what their lives have been like since leaving high school (1998). Some of the points in this paragraph have been conceptualized by Weis and Fine.

3. In her analysis of the white Freeway females' desires for further education, Weis (1990) notes that although statisticians who report on national trends often contend that today, more than 50 percent of high school graduates directly enroll in further education, the high number of students in her analysis who say they plan to go on for advanced studies does not necessarily reflect such numbers. Weis clarifies that such reports are often manipulated by "educational inflation," in which enrollment in four-year institutions, community colleges, and other tertiary-level schools—such as business institutes and cosmetology courses—are collapsed into one category.

4. Authors borrow categories from Howell (1972).

5. Weis et al. (1997) assert that the poor and working class white women in their study are involved in "meaningful networks" such as church groups and literacy centers, and as a result, do not necessarily reflect the experiences of those females who are most disengaged. Similarly, as the white Canal Town females are all regular participants in the neighborhood community center, they do not speak for those white girls that do not have "supportive" institutional connections.

6. Weis, Fine, and Marusza-Hall (1998) contend that the so-called cycle of violence may indeed be encouraged by living in a violent household, but, alternatively, may be largely produced because the violence goes unacknowledged, uninterrupted, and actively neglected by educators, clergy, family, neighbors, and friends.

7. This sophisticated way of looking at abuse is likely attributed to the extremely close relationship Hannah has with Ruby, who also serves as an informal counselor to these white youth.

8. Although the history of abuse in families and the frequency with which it occurs cannot be determined given the data, as Weis and Fine (1996) explain, if abuse was part of a parent's past, it will likely affect their parenting style and thus their children, even if there are no present instances of abuse.

9. I will further explore this point in Chapter 6.

10. In Proweller's (1995) exploration of the construction of female peer cultures in an upper-middle-class single-sex school, contextualized intersections of race and class generate a "polite" language of race which obscures any substantial discussion of structural inequity.

11. The authors contend that this more fluid sense of race exists in other Latin American countries, as does racism. In fact, Moore (1988) argues that racism in Cuba has historically rested upon the denigration of Africans.

12. I was not present during this discussion.

13. Personal communication with city bilingual education director, 1996.

CHAPTER 4. CANAL TOWN BOYS

1. The white Canal Town boys do not express much anger toward females of African and Puerto Rican descent. This does not suggest that they are not racist toward these females. Weis (1990), for example, found that the white Freeway boys placed African American females in the sexual realm, but only had disgust for these girls. In this study, the white Canal Town boys mostly ignore females from culturally oppressed groups, and likely focus their anger on males of African and Puerto Rican descent because they feel that they, unlike the females, are a considerable threat to their felt loss of privilege.

2. This point discussed in personal communication with Lois Weis.

3. The white Canal Town boys, like the girls, do not exhibit much resentment toward authority at the Center, and I theorize in subsequent chapters why I believe this to be the case.

4. Again, as noted in the previous chapter, although white working class girls and boys articulate a strong desire for further schooling, this can include a whole range of types of institutions—from research universities to business institutes (Weis, 1990).

5. These boys' responses may be mediated by their participation in the Saturday night anti-drug programming at the Center.

CHAPTER 5. THE BILINGUAL SCHOOL

1. Keller and Van Hooft (1982) remind that during the colonization of what came to be known as the United States and up until the middle of the nineteenth century, bilingual schooling was the norm, rather than the exception. Various voluntary and involuntary immigrant groups often formed their own schools, many of which were aligned with the group's religious denomination. In these schools, the native language was often used for instruction while English was taught as an academic subject.

2. Personal communication with city bilingual education director, 1996.

3. Personal communication with city bilingual education director, 1996.

4. There are no vice principals at this school.

5. Due to the nature of the hierarchy between administrators and teachers, it is not unusual for their relationship to be characterized by tension.

6. The white women and Puerto Rican women always sit at separate tables.

7. Female teacher aides, office personnel, and cafeteria staff of Puerto Rican descent are likely not part of the morning group because many of their duties begin early.

8. I never once observed a white office or cafeteria staff member spend time here. Also, the few front office personnel and cafeteria staff of African descent were never observed in any of the sites favored by the Puerto Rican or white women.

REFERENCES

Addelston, J., & Stirratt, M. (1996). The last bastion of masculinity: Gender politics and the construction of hegemonic masculinity at the Citadel. In C. Cheng (Ed.). *Masculinities and organizations*. Thousand Oaks, CA: Sage Publications.

Afulayan, J. (1993). Consequences of domestic violence on elementary school education. *Child and Family Therapy, 15 (3)*, 55–58.

American Colonization Society. (1835). *Minutes of the sixth session of the American Colonization Society, Buffalo, N.Y.*

Ani, M. (1994). *Yurugu: An African-centered critique of European cultural thought and behavior*. Trenton, NJ: African World Press.

Anyon, L. (1983). Workers, labor and economic history, and textbook context. In M. Apple & L. Weis (Eds.). *Ideology and practice in schooling*. Philadelphia: Temple University Press.

Apple, M. (1982). *Education and power*. London: Routledge and Kegan Paul.

Bilingual Education mimeo. (1990). *Buffalo Board of Education Bilingual Education Program*.

Bluestone, B., & Harrison, B. (1982). *The deindustrialization of America: Plant closings, community abandonment, and the dismantling of basic industry*. New York: Basic Books.

Board of Education mimeo. (1997). *Buffalo Board of Education Public School Statistics Information*.

Board of Education mimeo. (1975). *Buffalo Board of Education Public School Statistics Information*.

Bogdan, R., & Bilken, S. (1992). *Qualitative research for education: An introduction to theory and methods*. London: Allyn and Bacon.

Borman, K. (1998). *Ethnic diversity in communities and schools: Recognizing and building on strengths*. Stamford, CT: Ablex.

Borman, K., Mueninghoff, E., & Piazza, S. (1988). Urban Appalachian girls and young women: Bowing to no one. In L. Weis (Ed.). *Class, race, and gender in American education*. Albany: State University of New York Press.

Bourgois, P. (1995). *In search of respect: Selling crack in el barrio*. New York: Cambridge University Press.

Bowles, S., & Gintis, H. (1976). *Schooling in capitalist America*. New York: Basic Books.

Brown, B., & Theobald, W. (1998). Social institutions serving adolescents. In K. Borman & B. Schneider (Eds.). *The adolescent years: Social institutions and educational challenges*. Chicago: University of Chicago Press.

153

Brown, R., & Watson, B. (1981). *Buffalo: Lake city in Niagara land.* New York:

Bryan, B., Dadzie, S., & Scafe, S. (1985). *The heart of the race: Black women's lives in Britain.* London: Virago Press.

Burgess, R. (1991). Sponsors, gatekeepers, members and friends: Access in educational settings. In W. Shaffir & R. Stebbins (Eds.). *Experiencing fieldwork: An inside view of qualitative research.* Newbury Park: Sage Publications.

Butler, J. (1993). *Bodies that matter: On the discursive limits of "sex."* New York: Routledge.

Carby, H. (1982). White women listen! Black feminism and the boundaries of sisterhood. In *The empire strikes back: Race and racism in 70s Britain.* Birmingham: The Center for Contemporary Cultural Studies.

Carnoy, M. (1988). Education, state, and culture in American society. In H. Giroux & P. McLaren (Eds.). *Critical pedagogy, the state, and cultural struggle.* Albany: State University of New York Press.

Carrington, B. (1983). Sport as side-track: An analysis of West Indian involvement in extra-curricular sport. In S. Walker & L. Barton (Eds.). *Gender, class and education.* New York: Falmer Press.

Century Club. (1856). *Annual report of the Twentieth Century Club, Buffalo, New York.*

Charity Organization. (1855). *Twenty-ninth annual report of the Charity Organization Society of Buffalo, N.Y.*

Charity Organization. (1839). *Thirteenth annual report of the Charity Organization Society of Buffalo, N.Y.*

City of Buffalo (1843). *Nineteenth annual report of the superintendent of public schools for the city of Buffalo.*

Closson, F. (1894). The number of unemployed in Buffalo. *Publications of the Buffalo Historical Society.*

Common Council. (1897). *Proceedings of the Common Council of the city of Buffalo. From January 2, 1897 to December 31.*

Common Council. (1895). *Proceedings of the Common Council of the city of Buffalo. From January 2, 1895 to December 31.*

Connell, R. (1995). *Masculinities.* Berkeley: University of California Press.

Connell, R. (1993). Disruptions: Improper masculinities and schooling. In L. Weis & M. Fine (Eds.). *Beyond silenced voices: Class, race and gender in United States schools.* Albany: State University of New York Press.

Connell, R. (1987). *Gender and power.* Stanford, CA: Stanford University Press.

Coxe, A. (1874). *Buffalo notables and the war.* Buffalo: Sherman Home Press.

Crawford, J. (1989). *Bilingual education: History, politics, theory, and practice.* Trenton, NJ: Crane Publishing Company.

Crenshaw, K. (1989). Demarginalizing the intersection of race and sex: A Black feminist critique of antidiscrimination doctrine, feminist theory and antiracist politics. *University of Chicago Legal Forum, 89,* 139–167.

Dart, J. (1879). The grain elevators of Buffalo. *Publications of the Buffalo Historical Society, I.*

Davis, A. (1981). *Women, race and class.* New York: Vintage Books.

Devoy, J. (1896). *A history of the city of Buffalo.* Buffalo: The Times Press.

DeYoung, A. (1995). *The life and death of a rural American high school: Farewell Little Kanawha.* New York: Garland Publishing.

Donohue, T. (1895). *The Indians and the Jesuits.* Buffalo: Buffalo Catholic Publishing Company.

Eckert, P. (1989). *Jocks and burnouts: Social categories and identity in high school.* New York: Teachers College Press.

Elkind, P. (1984). *All grown up and no place to go.* Reading, MA: Addison Wesley.

Ellis, J. (Ed.). (1956). *Documents of Buffalo Catholic history.* Buffalo: The Holling Press.

Ellison, I. (1880). *The Germans in Buffalo. Publications of the Buffalo Historical Society.*

Evans, S., & Boyte, H. (1992). *Free spaces: The sources of democratic change in America.* New York: Harper & Row.

Everhart, R. (1983). *Reading, writing and resistance: Adolescence and labor in a junior high school.* Boston: Routledge and Kegan Paul.

Finders, M. (1996). *Just girls: Hidden literacies and life in junior high.* New York: Teachers College Press.

Fine, M., & Weis, L. (1998). *Voices of hope and despair.* New York: Beacon Press.

Fine, M., Weis, L., Addelston, J., & Marusza-Hall, J. (1997). (In)secure times: Constructing white working class masculine identities in the late 20th century. *Gender & Society, 11*, 52–68.

Foley, D. (1990). *Learning capitalist culture: Deep in the heart of Tejas.* Philadelphia: University of Pennsylvania Press.

Foote, W. (1943). *Street corner society: The social structure of an Italian slum.* Chicago: University of Chicago Press.

Frankenberg, R. (1993). *The social construction of whiteness: White women, race matters.* Minneapolis: University of Minnesota Press.

Friedrich, W., & Boriskin, J. (1976). The role of the child in abuse: A review of literature. *American Journal of Orthopsychiatry, 45*, 372–381.

Gelles, R., & Lancaster, J. (Eds.). (1987). *Child abuse and neglect: Biosocial dimensions.* New York: Aldine de Gruyter.

Gilmore, D. (1990). *Manhood in the making.* New Haven: Yale University Press.

Grant Agency Demographics. (1996).

Halle, D. (1984). *Work, home, and politics among blue-collar property owners.* Chicago: University of Chicago Press.

Heath, S., & McLaughlin, M. (Eds.). (1993). *Identity and inner-city youth: Beyond ethnicity and gender.* New York: Teachers College Press.

Hicks, E. (1981). Cultural Marxism: Non-synchrony and feminist practice. In L. Sargent (Ed.). *Women and revolution.* Boston: South End Press.

Hill, H. (1923). *Municipality of Buffalo, New York: A history, 1780–1923.* New York: Lewis Historical Publishing Company.

Hill, H. (1908). *An historical review of waterways and canal construction in New York State.* Buffalo: Buffalo Historical Society.

Hofstadter, R. (1944). *Social Darwinism in Buffalo, 1780–1923.* Unpublished manuscript.

Holland, D., & Eisenhart, M. (1990). *Educated in romance: Women, achievement, and college culture.* Chicago: University of Chicago Press.

Hosmer, G. (1880). *Physiognomy of Buffalo. Publications of the Buffalo Historical Society.*

Hotchkin, J. (1848). *A history of the purchase and settlement of Western New York, and of the rise, progress, and present state of the Presbyterian church in that section.* New York: M. W. Dodd.

Houghton, F. (1927). *Immigrant education: A hand book prepared for the board of education, Buffalo, New York.*

Howell, J. (1972). *Hard living on Clay Street: Portraits of blue collar families.* New York: Anchor Books.

Hubbell, M. (1896). *The charter of the city of Buffalo, from its incorporation in 1832 to 1896, inclusive.* Buffalo: The Wenborne-Sumner Company.

Hughes, H. (1988). Psychological and behavioral correlates of family violence in child witnesses and victims. *American Journal of Orthopsychiatry, 58,* 77–90.

Ignatiev, N. (1995). *How the Irish became white.* New York: Routledge.

Jaffe, P., Wolfe, S., & Wilson, S. (1990). *Children of battered women.* Newbury, Park: Sage.

Johnson, C. (1879). *The first school house in Buffalo. Publications of the Buffalo Historical Society.*

Jouriles, E., & Norwood, W. (1995). Physical aggression toward boys and girls in families characterized by the battering of women. *Journal of Family Psychology, 9 (1),* 69–78.

Justice, B., & Justice, R. (1990). *The abusing family.* New York: Plenum.

Keller, G., & Van Hooft, K. (1982). A chronology of bilingualism and bilingual education in the United States. In J. Fishman & G. Keller (Eds.). *Bilingual education for Hispanic students in the United States.* New York: Teachers College Press.

Ketchum, W. (1865). *An authentic and comprehensive history of Buffalo, with some account of its early inhabitants both savage and civilized, comprising historic notices of the six nations of Indians, including a sketch of the life of Sir William Johnson, and of other prominent white men.* Buffalo: Rockwell, Baker & Hill Printers.

Klein, A. (1993). *Little big men: Bodybuilding subculture and gender construction.* Albany: State University of New York Press.

Ladson-Billings, G. (1994). *The dreamkeepers: Successful teachers of African American children.* San Francisco: Jossey-Bass Publishers.

Lareau, A. (1989). *Home advantage: Social class and parental intervention in elementary education.* New York: The Falmer Press.

Larned, J. (1911). *A history of Buffalo.* New York: The Progress of the Empire State Company.

Liebow, E. (1967). *Tally's corner: A study of Negro street corner men.* Boston: Little, Brown.

London, H. (1978). *The culture of a community college.* New York: Praeger.

MacLeod, J. (1987). *Ain't no makin it: Leveled aspirations in a low-income neighborhood.* Boulder, CO: Westview Press.

Maynard, T. (1908). *Memorial and family history of early Buffalo*. Buffalo: The Genealogical Publishing Company.

McCarthy, C. (1990). *Race and curriculum: Social inequality and the theories and politics of difference in contemporary research on schooling*. New York: The Falmer Press.

McCarthy, C. (1988). Marxist theories of education and the challenge of a cultural politics of non-synchrony. In L. Roman, L. Christian-Smith & E. Ellsworth (Eds.). *Becoming feminine: The politics of popular culture*. New York: The Falmer Press.

McGroarty, M. (1992). The societal context of bilingual education. *Educational Researcher, 7*, 574–582.

McLaughlin, M., Irby, M., & Langman, J. (1994). *Urban sanctuaries: Neighborhood organizations in the lives and futures of inner-city youth*. San Francisco: Jossey-Bass Publishers.

McNeil, L. (1986). *Contradictions of control*. New York: Routledge and Kegan Paul.

McRobbie, A. (1978). Working class girls and the culture of femininity. In *The University of Birmingham, Center for Contemporary Cultural Studies: Women take issue*. London: Hutchinson.

Messner, M., & Sabo, D. (1994). *Sex, violence, and power in sports: Rethinking masculinity*. Freedom, CA: The Crossing Press.

Messner, M., & Sabo, D. (Eds.). (1990). *Sport, men, and the gender order: Critical feminist perspectives*. Champaign, IL: Human Kinetics Books.

Meyers, L. (1996). *Rethinking romance: Cultural construction of female gender identity at a prestigious, private university*. Unpublished doctoral dissertation, State University of New York at Buffalo.

Moore, C. (1988). *Castro, the Blacks, and Africa*. Center for Afro-American Studies: University of California, Los Angeles.

Muller, C., & Frisco, M. (1998). Working: Perceptions and experiences of American teenagers. In K. Borman & B. Schneider (Eds.). *The adolescent years: Social influences and educational challenges*. Chicago: University of Chicago Press.

Newman, F. (1998). Learning contexts beyond the classroom: Extracurricular activities, community organizations, and peer groups. In K. Borman & B. Schneider (Eds.). *The adolescent years: Social influences and educational challenges*. Chicago: University of Chicago Press.

Ogbu, J. (1988). Class stratification, racial stratification, and schooling. In L. Weis (Ed.). *Class, race, and gender in American education*. Albany: State University of New York Press.

O'Leary, S. (1870). *Hard times on the canal*. Unpublished manuscript.

O'Leary, S. (1863). *Life on the canal*. Unpublished manuscript.

Oliver, M., & Shapiro, T. (1995). *Black wealth, white wealth: A new perspective on racial inequality*. New York: Routledge.

Omi, M., & Winant, H. (1994). *Racial formation in the United States: From the 1960s to the 1990s*. New York: Routledge.

Padilla, F. (1985). *Latino ethnic consciousness: The case of Mexican Americans and Puerto Rican Americans in Chicago*. Notre Dame, IN: Notre Dame University Press.

Pedersen, G. (1956). *Early titles to Indian reservations in Western New York.* Lockport, NY: Niagara Frontier Publishers.

Perry, D. (Ed.). (1996). *Governance in Erie County: A foundation for understanding and action.* State University of New York at Buffalo: The Governance Project.

Perry, D. (1995). *Building the public city: The politics, governance, and finance of public infrastructure.* Thousand Oaks, CA: Sage Publications.

Peshkin, A. (1991). *The color of strangers, the color of friends: The play of ethnicity in school and community.* Chicago: University of Chicago Press.

Peshkin, A. (1986). *God's choice: The total world of a fundamentalist Christian school.* Chicago: University of Chicago Press.

Pleck, J., & Sawyer, J. (1974). *Men and masculinity.* Englewood Cliffs, NJ: Prentice-Hall.

Police Annuals. (1866). *Annual report of the board of police of the city of Buffalo for the year ending December 31, 1866.*

Police Annuals. (1865). *Annual report of the board of police of the city of Buffalo for the year ending December 31, 1865.*

Police Annuals. (1864). *Annual report of the board of police of the city of Buffalo for the year ending December 31, 1864.*

Police Annuals. (1863). *Annual report of the board of police of the city of Buffalo for the year ending December 31, 1863.*

Police Annuals. (1862). *Annual report of the board of police of the city of Buffalo for the year ending December 31, 1862.*

Police Annuals. (1843). *Annual report of the board of police of the city of Buffalo for the year ending December 31, 1843.*

Police Annuals. (1840). *Annual report of the board of police of the city of Buffalo for the year ending December 31, 1840.*

Police Annuals. (1838). *Annual report of the board of police of the city of Buffalo for the year ending December 31, 1838.*

Police Annuals. (1837). *Annual report of the board of police of the city of Buffalo for the year ending December 31, 1837.*

Polite, V. (1994). Reproduction and resistance: An analysis of African-American males' responses to schooling. In M. Shujaa (Ed.). *Too much schooling, too little education: A paradox of Black life in white societies.* Trenton, NJ: Africa World Press.

Polk, K. (1994). *When men kill: Scenarios of masculine violence.* London: Cambridge University Press.

Poole, M. (1905). Social life of Buffalo in the 30s and 40s. *Publications of the Buffalo Historical Society, VII.*

Proweller, A. (1995). *Inside absence: An ethnography of female identity construction in an upper middle-class youth culture.* Unpublished doctoral dissertation, State University of New York at Buffalo.

Raissiguier, C. (1994). *Becoming women, becoming workers: Identity formation in a French vocational school.* Albany: State University of New York Press.

Raphael, R. (1988). *The men from the boys.* London: Nebraska University Press.

Reid, J., Kavanaugh, B., & Baldwin, J. (1987). Abusive parents' perception of child problem behavior: An example of paternal violence. *Journal of Abnormal Child Psychology, 15*, 451–466.

Robins, D., & Cohen, P. (1978). *Knuckle sandwich*. New York: Penguin Books.

Roediger, D. (1994). *Towards the abolition of whiteness: Essays on race, politics, and working class history*. New York: Verso.

Roediger, D. (1991). *The wages of whiteness: Race and the making of the American working class*. New York: Verso.

Roman, L., Christian-Smith, L., & Ellsworth, E. (Eds.). (1988). *Becoming feminine: The politics of popular culture*. New York: The Falmer Press.

Sanday, P. (1990). *Fraternity gang rape: Sex, brotherhood, and privilege on campus*. New York: New York University Press.

Schneider, B., & Stevenson, D. (1999). *The ambitious generation: America's teenagers, motivated but directionless*. New Haven: Yale University Press.

Schneider, D. (1938). *The history of public welfare in Western New York, 1609–1866*. Chicago: University of Chicago Press.

Seeley Borden, A. (1998). *"Wiggers," "race traitors," and the politics of "posing": Constructions of whiteness in popular culture*. Unpublished master's thesis, University at Buffalo.

Sennett, R., & Cobb, J. (1972). *The hidden injuries of class*. New York: Knopf.

Severance, F. (1909). Historical sketch of the board of trade, the merchants' exchange and the chamber of commerce of Buffalo. *Publications of the Buffalo Historical Society, XIII*.

Severance, F. (1908). The Irish in early Buffalo. *Publications of the Buffalo Historical Society, XVI*.

Severance, F. (Ed.). (1907). Millard Fillmore Papers. *Publication of the Buffalo Historical Society, X*.

Shea, J. (1900). *Songs and romance in Buffalo*. Buffalo: Charles Wells Moulton, Publishers.

Smith, D. (1988). Femininity as discourse. In L. Roman, E. Christian-Smith, & E. Ellsworth, (Eds.). *Becoming feminine: The politics of popular culture*. London: The Falmer Press.

Smith, D. (1987). *The everyday world as problematic: A feminist sociology*. Boston: Northeastern University Press.

St. Clair, R., Valdes, G., & Ornstein-Galicia, J. (Eds.). (1981). *Social and educational issues in bilingualism and biculturalism*. Washington, DC: University Press of America.

Symons, T., & Quintus, J. (1902). History of Buffalo harbor. *Publications of the Buffalo Historical Society, V*.

Takaki, R. (1993). *A different mirror: A history of multicultural Ameica*. New York: Little, Brown.

Thomas, P. (1967). *Down these mean streets*. New York: Knopf.

Twentieth Century Club. (1854). *Annual report of the Twentieth Century Club, Buffalo, New York*.

Valli, L. (1988). Gender identity and the technology of office education. In L. Weis (Ed.). *Class, race, and gender in American education.* Albany: State University of New York Press.

Walker, J. (1987). *Louts and legends: Male youth culture in an inner city school.* London: Allen & Unwin.

Walter, F. (1958). *A social and cultural history of Buffalo, New York, 1865–1901.* Unpublished doctoral dissertation, Case Western Reserve, Cleveland, OH.

Weedon, C. (1987). *Feminist practice and poststructuralist theory.* New York: Basil Blackwell.

Weis, L., Marusza-Hall, J., & Fine, M. (1998). Out of the cupboard: Domestic violence and white poor and working class girls and women. *British Journal of Sociology of Education, 19 (1),* 53–73.

Weis, L., Centrie, C., Valentin-Juarbe, J., & Fine, M. (1997). "It's a small frog that will never leave Puerto Rico": Men and the struggle for place in the U.S. In M. Fine & L. Weis (Eds.). *Voices of hope and despair.* Boston: Beacon Press.

Weis, L., & Fine, M. (1996). *"The teacher would call me 'piggy,' 'smelly,' 'dirty,' names like that: Prying open a discussion of domestic violence for educators.* Unpublished manuscript.

Weis, L., Fine, M., Proweller, A., Bertram, C., & Marusza-Hall, J. (1996). I've slept in clothes long enough: Excavating the sounds of domestic violence among women in the white working class. *Urban Review, 30 (1),* 43–62.

Weis, L., & Fine, M. (1993). *Beyond silenced voices: Class, race, and gender in United States schools.* Albany: State University of New York Press.

Weis, L. (1990). *Working class without work.* New York: Routledge.

Weis, L. (1985). *Between two worlds: Black students in an urban community college.* New York: Routledge and Kegan Paul.

Wexler, P. (1988). Symbolic economy of identity and denial of labor: Studies in high school number 1. In L. Weis (Ed.). *Class, race, and gender in American education.* Albany: State University of New York Press.

Willis, P. (1977). *Learning to labor: How working class kids get working class jobs.* New York: Columbia University Press.

Wilson, W. (1990). *The truly disadvantaged: The inner city, the underclass and public policy.* Chicago: University of Chicago Press.

Wittke, C. (1956). *The Irish in America.* Baton Rouge: Louisiana State University Press.

Wittke, C. (1939). *We who built America.* New York: Prentice-Hall.

Woodson, C. (1933). *The mis-education of the Negro.* New York: AMS Press.

INDEX

academic performance, 39–40,
   63–66
Addelston, J., and Stirratt, M., 131
Aid to Families with Dependent
   Children (AFDC), 10, 34–35
Ani, M., 2, 13, 24, 52, 144
Anyon, J., 86
Apple, M., 4

bilingual school, 21, 40–41, 60–66,
   81–105; race/gender divisions
   94–105
Bluestone, B., and Harrison, B., 10,
   10
bordercrossers, 13
Borman, K., 3, 11
Borman, K., Mueninghoff, E., and
   Piazza, S., 9–10
Bourgois, P., 27
Bowles, S., and Gintis, H., 4
boys club, 129–130
Brown, B., and Theobald, W., 3, 11
Brown, R., and Watson, B., 16, 20
Bryan, B., Dadzie, S., and Scafe, S.,
   8–9
Burgess, R., 29

Canal Town, 1; history, 13–25
Canal Town Girls, 34–36, 37–57
Canal Town Boys, 34–36, 59–79
Carby, H., 51
Carnoy, M., 2
Carrington, B., 8, 9
Chapter I, 82
civil rights movement, 82
Closson, F., 19
community center, 29–31, 107–145;
   facilities, 109; schedule, 110; and

adults 107–109; history of
   109–110; staff 110–121; canal
   town girls, 121–126; canal town
   boys, 129–137
Connell, R., 59–60, 131
corporate connections, 118–121
Crawford, J., 82
Crenshaw, K., 2, 139

Dart, J., 18
data collection, 32–34
Davis, A., 144
Devoy, J., 15
DeYoung, A., 10
Donohue, T., 15

economy, 10, 18–19, 60
Elkind, P., 48
Ellis, J., 15, 19
Ellison, I., 15
Evans, S., and Boyte, H., 3, 10–13,
   107–109
Everhart, R., 2, 61

family wage, 2
female identity, 37; jobs and careers,
   38–41; education, 40–41; family,
   41–42; domestic violence, 41–48;
   racism, 40–41, 49–57
Finders, M., 2
Fine, M., and Weis, L., 11
Fine, M., Weis, L., Addelston, J.,
   Marusza-Hall, J., 59–60, 71, 131
Foley, D., 13
Foote, W., 10
Frankenberg, R., 9, 101
freespace, 3, 11–13,107–109
Friedrich, W., and Boriskin, J., 68